2012

A gift for:

Anne, Brian + family

From:

Mom Wear

Mons Day

More Joy
for the
Journey

A Woman's Book of Joyful Promises

Published by

THOMAS NELSON™

Since 1798

www.thomasnelson.com

More Joy for the Journey

Copyright © 2007 by Thomas Nelson, Inc.

Published in Nashville, Tennessee, by Thomas Nelson, Inc.

Thomas Nelson, Inc. titles may be purchased in bulk for educational, business, fundraising, or sales promotional use. For information, please e-mail SpecialMarkets@ThomasNelson.com.

Compiled and edited by Terri Gibbs

Unless otherwise indicated, all Scripture quotations in this book are from The New King James Version (NKJV) ©1979, 1980, 1982, 1992, 2002, Thomas Nelson, Inc., Publisher. Other Scripture references are from the following sources: *The New International Version of the Bible* (NIV) © 1984 by the International Bible Society. Used by permission of Zondervan Bible Publishers.

Designed by The DesignWorks Group, Sisters, Oregon.

ISBN-10: 1-4041-0327-9
ISBN-13: 978-1-4041-0327-6

www.thomasnelson.com

Printed and bound in China

CONTENTS

MORE JOY
FOR THE JOURNEY

FINDING JOY IN GOD'S LOVE

PART ONE

Living in complete joy
requires living in complete
confidence in God.

DEE BRESTIN

[Jesus] went to the Pharisee's house, and sat down to eat. And behold, a woman in the city who was a sinner, when she knew that Jesus sat at the table in the Pharisee's house, brought an alabaster flask of fragrant oil, and stood at His feet behind Him weeping; and she began to wash His feet with her tears, and wiped them with the hair of her head; and she kissed His feet and anointed them with the fragrant oil. Now when the Pharisee who had invited Him saw this, he spoke to himself, saying, "This Man, if He were a prophet, would know who and what manner of woman this is who is touching Him, for she is a sinner." . . . Then [Jesus] turned to the woman and said to Simon, "Do you see this woman? I entered your house; you gave Me no water for My feet, but she has washed My feet with her tears and wiped them with the hair of her head. You gave Me no kiss, but this woman has not ceased to kiss My feet since the time I came in. You did not anoint My head with oil, but this woman has anointed My feet with fragrant oil. Therefore I say to you, her sins, which are many, are forgiven, for she loved much."

LUKE 7:36–50

10

THE JOY OF GOD'S LOVE

*t*he nameless woman from Nain heard that Jesus, the Jewish rabbi, was to dine at Simon the Pharisees home that evening. A notoriously sinful woman, she was sought by Nain's men in the darkest hours of their lustiest nights. To satisfy their illicit sexual cravings, they used her and abused her. . . .

The nameless woman from Nain, however, had come to a turning point in her life. She gazed into the mirror of her soul and could not bear her own reflection. She realized her sinfulness. She craved the forgiveness and peace offered by the popular teacher from Nazareth.

She arrives at Simon's house while Jesus is eating there. . . . She darts to Him and collapses at His feet and cries. Her actions sketch the scene of her sinful nature. Her hair cleanses Christ's feet as she yearns for Him to cleanse her heart. . . . Her alabaster bottle of perfume, poured on His toes, pays tribute to the power of His future resurrection and to His divine kingship. . . .

Jesus states, "Her many sins have been forgiven— for she loved much."

DENISE GEORGE
Cultivating a Forgiving Heart

PROMISES ABOUT
GOD'S TENDER CARE

Are not two sparrows sold for a copper coin?
And not one of them falls to the
ground apart from your Father's will.

MATTHEW 10:29

[Cast] all your care upon Him,
for He cares for you.

1 PETER 5:7

Bless the LORD, O my soul,
and forget not all His benefits:
Who forgives all your iniquities,
Who heals all your diseases,
Who redeems your life from destruction,
Who crowns you with lovingkindness
and tender mercies.

PSALM 107:2−4

God's Tender Care

*e*nglish sparrows. They're worth barely a penny, Jesus said so. Yet of the world's nine thousand bird species, Jesus singled out the least-noticed and most insignificant of birds to make a point.

If God takes time to keep tabs on every sparrow—who it is, where it's going, whether or not its needs are being met—then surely He keeps special tabs on you. Intimately. Personally. And with every detail in mind.

The Bible may point to eagles to underscore courage and power, and it may talk about doves as symbols of peace and contentment. But God's Word reserves sparrows to teach a lesson about trust. Just as God tenderly cares for a tiny bird, even making note of when it is harmed, or when it falls to the ground, He gently reminds you that He is worthy of your greatest trust, your deepest confidence.

JONI EARECKSON TADA
Diamonds in the Dust

PROMISES ABOUT
GOD'S PERFECT PLAN

*God is my strength and power, and He
makes my way perfect.*

2 SAMUEL 22:33

*How precious also are Your thoughts to me,
O God!
How great is the sum of them!
If I should count them,
they would be more in number than the sand.*

PSALM 139:17–18

*I know the thoughts that I think toward you,
says the LORD, thoughts of peace and not of evil,
to give you a future and a hope.*

JEREMIAH 29:11

God's Perfect Plan

*g*od has been making arrangements for your part in His plan long before you were born. He is never unprepared.

Your past does not surprise Him.

Your present does not worry Him.

Your future is not a mystery to Him.

No one is a second-class laborer in His harvest. You are precious to Him. He is the Almighty, you are His beloved child, and we are all part of the wonderful tapestry of His eternal purposes.

ALICIA BRITT CHOLE

Pure Joy

PROMISES ABOUT
BEING SAFE IN GOD'S LOVE

*In all their affliction He was afflicted,
and the Angel of His Presence saved them;
in His love and in His pity He redeemed them;
and He bore them and carried them
all the days of old.*

ISAIAH 63:9

*God has not given us a spirit of fear,
but of power and
of love and of a sound mind.*

2 TIMOTHY 1:7

*In the time of trouble
He shall hide me in His pavilion.*

PSALM 27:5

SAFE IN GOD'S LOVE

*t*here is an incredible painting by the Spanish artist Sorolla that depicts a man dressed in a priestly white gown standing before a group of lepers. His arms are raised, and the expression on his face is a mixture of anger and compassion. He faces a crowd of children that is ready to hurl sticks and rocks at the lepers huddled behind him. The priest stands in the gap as a human shield. . . .

Jesus stood in the gap for us. He was willing to come up against all the negative forces in the world and tell us, in effect, "Get behind me and they cannot affect you. I will absorb and deflect the harm."

LAURIE BETH JONES
Jesus in Blue Jeans

PROMISES ABOUT
GOD'S FORGIVENESS OF SIN

*In Him we have redemption through His blood,
the forgiveness of sins,
according to the riches of His grace.*

EPHESIANS 1:7

*If we walk in the light as He is in the light,
we have fellowship with one another,
and the blood of Jesus Christ His Son
cleanses us from all sin.*

1 JOHN 1:7

*If we confess our sins, He is faithful
and just to forgive us our sins and to cleanse us
from all unrighteousness.*

1 JOHN 1:9

*Create in me a clean heart, O God,
and renew a steadfast spirit within me.*

PSALM 51:10

GOD FORGIVES AND FORGETS

*i*t's been said that there is only one thing God cannot do, and that is to remember your sin and mine that has been forgiven. When I come to Him humbly, through faith in Jesus, He erases my sin from His memory much more effectively than I erase things from my computer. Even Satan can't retrieve it from the inner workings of my spiritual hard drive!

Corrie ten Boom, author of *The Hiding Place* and survivor of the Nazi concentration camps during World War II, once remarked that God has cast our sins into the depths of the sea and posted a sign that says, "No Fishing Allowed."

ANNE GRAHAM LOTZ
I Saw the Lord

PROMISES ABOUT
GOD'S UNFAILING LOVE

*As high as the heavens are above the earth, so
great is his love for those who fear him.*

PSALM 103:11 NIV

*In this the love of God was manifested toward us,
that God has sent His only begotten Son
into the world, that we might live through Him.
In this is love, not that we loved God,
but that He loved us and sent His Son to be
the propitiation for our sins.*

1 JOHN 4:9, 10

*Because Your lovingkindness is better than life,
my lips shall praise You.
Thus I will bless You while I live;
I will lift up my hands in Your name.*

PSALM 63:3–4

GOD'S UNFAILING LOVE

*t*here are two kinds of love: human love and God's love. Human love can fall short; God's love never does. . . .

I experienced that love when I was imprisoned in a concentration camp during the Second World War. Each morning they held roll call. The supervisor used that time to demonstrate her cruelty. One morning I could hardly bear to see and hear what was happening in front of me. Then a lark started to sing in the air. All the prisoners looked up. I looked up too and listened to the bird, but I looked further and saw heaven. I thought of Psalm 103:11, "For as high as the heavens are above the earth, so great is his love for those who fear him" (NIV). I suddenly saw that the ocean of God's great love is greater than human cruelty. God sent the lark every day for three weeks to teach us to direct our eyes to Him.

CORRIE TEN BOOM
Messages of God's Abundance

PROMISES ABOUT
GOD'S NEVER-ENDING LOVE

Therefore know that the LORD your God,
He is God, the faithful God who
keeps covenant and mercy for a thousand
generations with those who love Him
and keep His commandments.

DEUTERONOMY 7:9

"The Father Himself loves you,
because you have loved Me, and have believed
that I came forth from God."

JOHN 16:27

The LORD has appeared of old to me, saying:
"Yes, I have loved you with an
everlasting love; therefore with
lovingkindness I have drawn you."

JEREMIAH 31:3

God's Never-Ending Love

*h*ave you heard the story of the old woman whose life had been a constant struggle against poverty, and who had never seen the ocean? On being taken to the seaside for the first time, she exclaimed, "Thank God there's something there's enough of!"

Scripture is one long, beautiful story of God's patient, perfect, lavish love for humankind. . . . Sometimes His love doesn't look the way we want it to at the moment; . . . but His grace is ever-present and His love is never-ending.

It's been said that the Christian life is like the dial of a clock. The hands are God's hands, passing over and over again, the short hand of discipline and the long hand of mercy. . . . And the hands are fastened to one secure pivot: the great, unchanging heart of our God of love.

Now that's something there's always more than enough of!

BARBARA JOHNSON
Boundless Love

PROMISES ABOUT
GOD'S GRACE

*In Him we have redemption through
His blood, the forgiveness of sins,
according to the riches of His grace.*

EPHESIANS 1:7

*You were not redeemed with corruptible things,
like silver or gold, from your aimless conduct
received by tradition from your fathers,
but with the precious blood of Christ, as of a lamb
without blemish and without spot.*

1 PETER 1:18–19

*He has not dealt with us according to our sins,
nor punished us according to our iniquities.
For as the heavens are high above the earth,
so great is His mercy toward those who fear Him;
as far as the east is from the west,
so far has He removed our transgressions from us.*

PSALM 103:10–12

God's Great Grace

When my friend Karen returned from England she told me about visiting the Tower of London and beholding the stunning crown jewels of Great Britain.

"I asked an attentive and well-accented Beefeater about the value of the crown jewels," she told me, "and instead of an answer, I received an education."

The guard explained . . . that the jewels lend their splendor to coronations and jubilees as symbols of royalty, authority, justice, and spirituality. They remain a tangible link, he said, between modern-day England and the kings and queens of long ago. . . . As to stated value, the storied jewels have none. That's hard to believe until you ask, How could you put a price on such magnificence? . . . They are irreplaceable and without comparison; no price tag could do them justice.

So it is with grace. . . . Grace has no equal and its value goes far beyond imagery, history, and tradition.

JENNIFER ROTHSCHILD
Lessons I Learned in the Light

PROMISES ABOUT
GOD'S PRESENCE

He Himself has said,
"I will never leave you nor forsake you."
HEBREWS 13:5

"Lo, I am with you always,
even to the end of the age."
MATTHEW 28:20

Where can I go from Your Spirit?
Or where can I flee from Your presence?
If I ascend into heaven, You are there;
if I make my bed in hell, behold, You are there.
If I take the wings of the morning,
and dwell in the uttermost parts of the sea,
even there Your hand shall lead me,
and Your right hand shall hold me.
PSALM 139:7–10

FILLED WITH GOD HIMSELF

*i*f I were God, I don't think I would let any of my male servants close to a woman of Rahab's chosen profession. But while I would only look at the circumstances of her life, God saw this woman's heart. Rahab hid the Israelite spies in her home, and in turn God protected her family and allowed them to live with the Israelite people. And Rahab became a great-great-multiplied-times-great grandmother of Jesus Himself.

So what are God's qualifications to be used by Him and to have an up-close, personal relationship with Him? I think there's just one. "Man looks at the outward appearance, but the LORD looks at the heart" (1 Samuel 16:7). God is looking for devoted hearts, repentant hearts, hearts that are willing to be emptied of self and filled with Him.

SHARON JAYNES AND LYSA TERKUERST
A Woman's Secret to a Balanced Life

PROMISES ABOUT
GOD OUR PROVIDER

God is our refuge and strength,
a very present help in trouble.

PSALM 46:1

He gives power to the weak,
and to those who have
no might He increases strength.

ISAIAH 40:29

Surely He has borne our griefs
and carried our sorrows.

ISAIAH 53:4

We do not have a High Priest
who cannot sympathize with our weaknesses,
but was in all points tempted as we are,
yet without sin. Let us therefore come boldly
to the throne of grace, that we may obtain mercy
and find grace to help in time of need.

HEBREWS 4:15–17

God Is Our Provider

*t*here's nothing quite like the satisfaction of a glass of cold spring water on a hot . . . afternoon. A cold shower after mowing the lawn. A dive into a stream after a long, tiring hike. Sometimes a glass of lemonade fresh out of the refrigerator. Being satisfied means you've been filled, you want nothing more, and that the thirsty longing has been quenched.

That's exactly how Jesus satisfies. To have Him means that you have it all. To trust Him means that your needs are met. To know Him is to realize that He is your dearest, most faithful companion. . . .

The next time you pour a cold drink on a hot . . . afternoon, pause and praise the Lord for the way He quenches your thirst. He, the Wellspring of Water, overcomes, subdues, fulfills, and satisfies like nothing else, like no one else.

JONI EARECKSON TADA

Diamonds in the Dust

FINDING JOY IN A
POSITIVE ATTITUDE

PART TWO

*One way to develop the joyful habit
is to nurture an attitude
of thankfulness.*

BARBARA JOHNSON

Mordecai had brought up Hadassah, that is, Esther, his uncle's daughter, for she had neither father nor mother. The young woman was lovely and beautiful. When her father and mother died, Mordecai took her as his own daughter.

So it was, when the king's command and decree were heard, and when many young women were gathered at Shushan the citadel, under the custody of Hegai, that Esther also was taken to the king's palace, into the care of Hegai the custodian of the women. Now the young woman pleased him, and she obtained his favor; so he readily gave beauty preparations to her, besides her allowance. . . .

So Esther was taken to King Ahasuerus, into his royal palace, in the tenth month, which is the month of Tebeth, in the seventh year of his reign. The king loved Esther more than all the other women, and she obtained grace and favor in his sight more than all the virgins; so he set the royal crown upon her head and made her queen instead of Vashti.

ESTHER 2:7–9; 16–17

THE JOY OF A POSITIVE ATTITUDE

*i*n the Old Testament we can read the story of Esther. Her history had been one of sorrow and loss. Caught up in the captivity, she found herself chosen to compete in a beauty queen contest. She had no choice at all in the matter. After all, she was a foreign slave—and she was a woman! Suddenly, her entire future was determined, and her own dreams of marriage and family were undoubtedly dashed. What thoughts went through her mind when she was chosen to be queen of Persia? Even as royalty, Esther would be forced to play out a role she'd had no role in creating.

Esther—whose name means "star"—could have hung up her joy early on when she was orphaned and taken prisoner, but she didn't. She sang a song of purity, piety, and poise that made her captors gasp. It was her sweet song of Zion spirituality. Although her masters understood it only dimly, her song won her the queen's crown. . . . Esther persevered. She refused to be or do anything less than her best for the God she served.

JILL BRISCOE
Heartstrings

PROMISES ABOUT HAVING
A GOOD OUTLOOK ON LIFE

One thing I do, forgetting those things
which are behind and reaching forward
to those things which are ahead,
I press toward the goal for the prize of the
upward call of God in Christ Jesus.

PHILIPPIANS 3:13–14

Now to Him who is able to keep you
from stumbling, and to present you faultless
before the presence of His glory
with exceeding joy, to God our Savior,
Who alone is wise, be glory and majesty,
dominion and power, both now and forever.

JUDE 24–25

I thank my God upon every remembrance of you,
. . . being confident of this very thing,
that He who has begun a good work in you will
complete it until the day of Jesus Christ.

PHILIPPIANS 1:3–6

A Good Outlook on Life

i smiled when I read the poster in the window of the mall beauty salon: "It's never too late to be what you might have been." It was surrounded by pictures of the latest hairstyles and colors. I guess that was supposed to be the message: It's never too late to be a blond if that's what you know you are deep inside! . . .

I think it's a wonderful statement and a spiritual truth. In God it's never too late to be what you might have been. So many people walk through life with regret. That seems like such a wasted, draining emotion to me. We are not powerless in our lives to make a change, to start over again, to learn to do better next time.

There is so much in life that is wonderful, and it's not too late to grab hold of it.

SHEILA WALSH

The Best Devotions of Sheila Walsh

PROMISES ABOUT
CHOOSING A JOYFUL ATTITUDE

Whatever things are true,
whatever things are noble, whatever things are
just, whatever things are pure,
whatever things are lovely, whatever things
are of good report, if there is any virtue
and if there is anything praiseworthy—
meditate on these things.

PHILIPPIANS 4:8

Do not sorrow,
for the joy of the LORD is your strength.

NEHEMIAH 8:10

Blessed are the people who know
the joyful sound! They walk, O LORD, in the
light of Your countenance.

PSALM 89:15

CHOOSING A JOYFUL ATTITUDE

i remember, years ago when we lived in England, putting my children to bed one night. My husband was in Australia—literally on the other side of the world. He wasn't coming home for three long, hard months. My father had been diagnosed with cancer, my daughter had fallen and broken her arm the day my husband left, and my hands were more than full, running a preschool during the day and programs for dozens of needy teenagers in the evenings. (During this time it didn't help to catch mumps from my kids either!) Yet as I sat by the crackling fire in our tiny home, a huge sense of well-being invaded every corner of my life. . . . My heart was singing, and my soul was dancing. . . .

I have learned to accept what God allows and to change what He empowers me to change; and that's usually my own attitude.

JILL BRISCOE
Heartstrings

PROMISES ABOUT
GUARDING YOUR THOUGHTS

Know the God of your father, and serve
Him with a loyal heart and with a willing mind;
for the LORD searches all hearts
and understands all the intent of the thoughts.

1 CHRONICLES 28:9

Commit your works to the LORD,
and your thoughts will be established.

PROVERBS 16:3

For the word of God is living and powerful,
and sharper than any two-edged sword,
piercing even to the division of soul and spirit,
and of joints and marrow, and is a discerner of
the thoughts and intents of the heart.

HEBREWS 4:12

GUARDING THE GATES TO OUR MINDS

i love gates, especially well-tended ones. They suggest preparedness, privilege, and privacy. And gates give me a sense of adventure, especially when I swing open a gate and discover a path to follow. If you have a brick path that leads to a covered porch with a waiting cushioned rocker, honey, I'm your newest houseguest. . . .

When I consider the significance of a gate . . . I can't help but think about the gate that opens into our minds. Our minds have the capacity for reasoning, creativity, and foolishness. It's that last one that throws the monkey wrench into the mechanism. I've learned through the years that thoughts are powerful forces that can influence our health, our attitudes, and our relationships with others and with God. Therefore, we must tend to the gates within ourselves.

PATSY CLAIRMONT
Mending Your Heart in a Broken World

PROMISES TO HELP YOU
OVERCOME DREARY DAYS

*Thanks be to God, who gives us the victory
through our Lord Jesus Christ.*

1 CORINTHIANS 15:57

*May our Lord Jesus Christ Himself,
and our God and Father, who has loved us
and given us everlasting consolation and
good hope by grace, comfort your hearts
and establish you in every good word and work.*

2 THESSALONIANS 2:16–17

*Be glad in the LORD and rejoice, you righteous;
and shout for joy, all you upright in heart!*

PSALM 32:11

OVERCOMING DREARY DAYS

While flying to a conference recently, I was leafing through the airline's magazine, which has items you can purchase through a catalog. I spied a darling ad showing a black umbrella. The description said, "Gray skies are gonna clear up!" The umbrella opened to reveal a blue sky with white fluffy clouds floating by. It was like moving out from under dismal rain clouds to a clear bright day at the touch of a button.

I had to order that umbrella, of course, because it was such an encouragement to me! When it arrived in the mail, it was even better than depicted in the advertisement. . . .

None of us can avoid the gray skies and dreariness in life. At times we get absolutely drenched with troubles. But you know what? They're gonna clear up! Nothing lasts forever. The stuff we go through is only temporary. There will be lots of clearings along the way. And one day we will enjoy blue skies forever.

BARBARA JOHNSON
Extravagant Grace

*Oh come, let us sing to the LORD! Let us shout
joyfully to the Rock of our salvation.*

PSALM 95:1

*The humble also shall
increase their joy in the LORD.*

ISAIAH 29:19

*The ransomed of the LORD shall return,
and come to Zion with singing,
with everlasting joy on their heads.
They shall obtain joy and gladness,
and sorrow and sighing shall flee away.*

ISAIAH 35:10

Our Eternal Joy

*i*n Chaim Potok's novel *My Name Is Asher Lev*, a famous painter defines whether or not one is an artist by "whether or not there is a scream in him wanting to get out in a special way." His friend then immediately adds, "Or a laugh." Pondering that bit of dialogue I realize with repentance and with rapture that Christians have both. God's people know the scream, for it is painful to acknowledge that all flesh is grass and to live in its withered failures. We weep with the world's sorrows of brokenness and faded dreams.

But Christians also can't help but laugh. We laugh with victory over despair. We laugh eternally. We bubble with delight because we are God's children. We giggle in the freedom of divine approval. The promise stands forever that grace is the foundation of the world and undergirds our lives. God's eternal Word assures us of eternal life with Him—already begun.

MARVA DAWN
To Walk and Not Faint

PROMISES TO
REMIND YOU OF GOD'S LOVE

*He chose us in Him before the foundation of the
world, that we should be holy and without
blame before Him in love, having predestined us
to adoption as sons by Jesus Christ to Himself,
according to the good pleasure of His will,
to the praise of the glory of His grace, by which
He made us accepted in the Beloved.*

EPHESIANS 1:4–6

*O LORD, You have searched me and known me;
You know my sitting down and my rising up;
You understand my thought afar off.
You comprehend my path and my lying down,
and are acquainted with all my ways.*

PSALM 139:1–3

*Your hands have made me and fashioned me;
give me understanding,
that I may learn Your commandments.*

PSALM 119:73

LOVED AND MADE BY GOD

One of my favorite television commercials has no words. A young woman walks into a shop and admires a bathing suit on a mannequin. With a look of self-satisfaction, she picks up a suit like it, disappears into a dressing room, throws her own clothes over the door, then, after a couple seconds, lets out a blood-curdling scream. It's a powerhouse endorsement of the diet the commercial recommends. I laugh every time I see it as I munch away on my Snickers. . . .

The next time you stand in front of a mirror and want to scream, try to remember that God made that face. That smile. Those big eyes . . . and chubby cheeks. You are His creation, called to reflect Him. Spiritual transformation doesn't come from a diet program, a bottle, a makeover, or mask. It comes from an intimate relationship with the Savior. He . . . appreciates us for who we really are. So we can, too.

LUCI SWINDOLL
Extravagant Grace

45

Be of good courage,
and He shall strengthen your heart,
all you who hope in the LORD.

PSALM 31:24

Why are you cast down, O my soul?
And why are you disquieted within me?
Hope in God; for I shall yet praise Him, the help
of my countenance and my God.

PSALM 42:11

I will hope continually,
and will praise You yet more and more.

PSALM 71:14

It is good that one should hope and
wait quietly for the salvation of the LORD.

LAMENTATIONS 3:26

Planting Hope

ive years ago I planted over 300 bulbs around a brick pathway and in varying places in our yard. I told my husband that I'd be able to manage the winter somehow if I could look forward to a spring and summertime filled with the vibrant colors of crocuses, daffodils, tulips, snowdrops, and lilies.

In a sense, I planted hope. The hope of new life. The products of sun and warmth.

When I feel my spirits drooping, I . . . envision all the lovely red, white, purple, pink, orange, and blue flowers that will explode in a wild proliferation of joy all over my yard, come spring.

When I can't find hope, hope has an exquisite way of finding me . . . through the promises of what will be.

JULIE ANN BARNHILL
Exquisite Hope

PROMISES ABOUT
YOUR WONDERFUL UNIQUENESS

Your hands have made me and fashioned me;
give me understanding,
that I may learn Your commandments.

PSALM 119:73

God has dealt to each one a measure of faith.
For as we have many members in one body,
but all the members do not have the
same function, so we, being many, are one body
in Christ, and individually members of one
another. Having then gifts differing according to
the grace that is given to us, let us use them.

ROMANS 12:3—6

You are He who took Me out of the womb;
You made Me trust while on My mother's breasts.
I was cast upon You from birth.
From My mother's womb
You have been My God.

PSALM 22:9—10

Uniquely You

When I was growing up and obsessing about the size of my nose (substantial), my grandmother used to tell me, "It gives you character." I distinctly recall thinking that I could've done with a little less "character." She would also remind me in my insecure moments that people were not thinking about me as much as I imagined they were. She said that they were all doing the same thing I was doing: wondering what others were thinking of *them*. If I could reclaim a chunk of lost time and wasted emotional energy, I would wish to have back all the moments I spent lost in those useless thoughts.

If beauty is in the eye of the beholder, your wonderful uniqueness is precisely what brings God pleasure. It gives you "character," and He's smitten with you. So don't just embrace your uniqueness; revel in it.

ANITA RENFROE
The Purse-Driven Life

I will give thanks to You, O LORD,
among the Gentiles,
and sing praises to Your name.

2 SAMUEL 22:50

The LORD is great and greatly to be praised;
He is also to be feared above all gods.

1 CHRONICLES 16:25

The LORD is my strength and my shield;
my heart trusted in Him, and I am helped;
therefore my heart greatly rejoices,
and with my song I will praise Him.

PSALM 28:7

Hearts Set to Singing

a smile on your heart means a smile on your face. Some people wear their hearts on their sleeves. What goes on inside, shows up outside. Have you ever asked a junior-high daughter to help you with the housework? Her face tells the story. Her heart is definitely not in it!

When your heart has Jesus as its guest, it smiles. How can it do anything else? When your heart houses the one who is our joy, it cannot help grinning at grief, laughing at loads, and smiling at sorrows. Even when we are called to suffer, we cannot be sad or sour because we discover that we have been saved to sing. . . .

"But" you may object, "how can I even smile when I'm suffering, much less sing about it?" Look at Jesus! Can you look at Jesus and remain sober? When I'm in trouble, and I meet Him in the secret place and He smiles at me, that mends my heart so I can mend others. He sets my heart singing.

JILL BRISCOE
Quiet Times with God

PROMISES TO
HELP YOU PRAISE GOD

Why are you cast down, O my soul?
And why are you disquieted within me?
Hope in God; for I shall yet praise Him, the help
of my countenance and my God.

PSALM 43:5

The LORD is my rock and my fortress and
my deliverer; my God, my strength,
in whom I will trust; my shield and the
horn of my salvation, my stronghold. I will call
upon the LORD, who is worthy to be praised;
so shall I be saved from my enemies.

PSALM 18:2–3

I will call upon the LORD,
who is worthy to be praised;
so shall I be saved from my enemies.

2 SAMUEL 22:4

SINGING GOD'S PRAISES

*a*s a little girl, I would sing all the time in the privacy of my great-grandparents' little back alley apartment. I would sing old hymns and choruses like "Nearer My God to Thee," "What a Friend We Have in Jesus," and "Jesus Loves Me, This I know." I'd sing those songs and feel something swelling up in my spirit. I didn't know what it was, but my eyes would begin to fill up and tears would run down my round cheeks. This emotion, this exuberance, this *Presence* would overpower me. It was like a celebration in my heart. It was a party! . . .

Most of the time, as soon as my feet hit the floor in the morning, I turn on praise music. I love gospel music; it gets me going! . . . There's something about listening to praise music that opens up the portals of heaven on earth and reassures me that I'm surrounded by God's loving presence.

My great-grandmother used to sing, "I woke up this morning with my mind stayed on Jesus." . . . Let's praise Him in the morning, praise Him in the noon day, and praise Him in the evening.

THELMA WELLS
Boundless Love

PROMISES TO HELP YOU
DREAM BIG DREAMS

*Whatever you ask in My name,
that I will do, that the Father may be
glorified in the Son.*

JOHN 14:13

The plans of the diligent lead surely to plenty.

PROVERBS 21:5

*Great is our LORD, and mighty in power;
His understanding is infinite.*

PSALM 147:5

*It will be recounted of the LORD to the
next generation, they will come and declare His
righteousness to a people who will be born,
that He has done this.*

PSALM 22:30

LET YOUR DREAMS TAKE WINGS

Why are swings so incredibly delightful? Remember the day when you suddenly realized you didn't have to be pushed to swing, that you could propel yourself through the air by pumping your legs? Ahh, what freedom!

Swings give a feeling of weightlessness—for a few moments you bypass the laws of gravity. For a few moments you fly!

Dreams do much the same thing. Dreams crash the confines of what is and what has been. As our minds dare to see the unseen, our imagination fuels our faith and we begin to trust God for something more.

Some folks are afraid to dream. But connected to God, it is safe to dream. There is freedom to let faith take wings.

ALICIA BRITT CHOLE

Pure Joy

PROMISES ABOUT
OUR CELESTIAL HOME

Eye has not seen, nor ear heard . . .
the things which God has
prepared for those who love Him.

1 CORINTHIANS 2:9

If I go and prepare a place for you,
I will come again and receive you to Myself;
that where I am, there you may be also.

JOHN 14:3

God will wipe away every tear from their eyes;
there shall be no more death, nor sorrow,
nor crying. There shall be no more pain, for the
former things have passed away.
Then He who sat on the throne said,
"Behold, I make all things new."

REVELATION 21:4–5

Sights on the Celestial City

*L*et's be honest. Old age entails suffering. I'm acutely aware of this now as I watch my mother, once so alive and alert and quick, now so quiet and confused and slow. She suffers. We who love her suffer. We see the "preview of coming attractions," ourselves in her shoes, and ponder what this interval means in terms of the glory of God in an old woman. . . .

We look at what's happening—limitations of hearing, seeing, moving, digesting, remembering; distortions of countenance, figure, and perspective. If that's all we could see, we'd certainly want a face-lift or something.

But we're on a pilgrim road. It's rough and steep, and it winds uphill to the very end. We can lift up our eyes and see the unseen: a Celestial City, a light, a welcome, an ineffable Face. We shall behold Him. We shall be like Him. And that makes a difference in how we go about aging.

ELISABETH ELLIOT
On Asking God Why

FINDING JOY IN GENEROSITY AND LOVE

PART THREE

*God works through us to meet the needs
of those around us.*

JOANIE YODER

The scribes and Pharisees brought to [Jesus] a woman caught in adultery. And when they had set her in the midst, they said to Him, "Teacher, this woman was caught in adultery, in the very act. Now Moses, in the law, commanded us that such should be stoned. But what do You say?" This they said, testing Him, that they might have something of which to accuse Him. But Jesus stooped down and wrote on the ground with His finger, as though He did not hear.

So when they continued asking Him, He raised Himself up and said to them, "He who is without sin among you, let him throw a stone at her first." And again He stooped down and wrote on the ground. . . . When Jesus had raised Himself up and saw no one but the woman, He said to her, "Woman, where are those accusers of yours? Has no one condemned you?"

She said, "No one, Lord."

And Jesus said to her, "Neither do I condemn you; go and sin no more."

JOHN 8:3–11

THE JOY OF
GENEROSITY AND LOVE

When the Scribes and the Pharisees brought the woman taken in adultery to Jesus for judgment, He knelt down and began to draw in the sand. I'm convinced He did not draw a straight line, demarcating "On this side are the sinners—on this side are the saints." He said, "Whoever is without sin among you may cast the first stone," and then He began to draw in circles—circles that took in all their sins—circles that surrounded all of them with love.

What goes around, comes around. When we dispense mercy, we receive mercy. When we give value, we receive value in return.

LAURIE BETH JONES
Jesus in Blue Jeans

PROMISES ABOUT
GIVING MERCY AND FORGIVENESS

Peter came to Him and said,
"Lord, how often shall my brother sin against me,
and I forgive him? Up to seven times?"
Jesus said to him, "I do not say to you, up to
seven times, but up to seventy times seven."

MATTHEW 18:21—22

Whenever you stand praying,
if you have anything against anyone,
forgive him, that your Father in heaven may
also forgive you your trespasses.

MARK 11:25

Judge not, and you shall not be judged.
Condemn not, and you shall not be condemned.
Forgive, and you will be forgiven.

LUKE 6:37

GIVING MERCY
AND FORGIVENESS

*m*ay I just say something and get it out into the open? We're all dysfunctional. There isn't one of us who hasn't "functioned abnormally" at some point in time. There isn't one of us who has skated through life without an impairment of some sort tagging behind her. . . .

Listen: I struggle. I dream. I aspire to be more like Jesus.

And on other days? Well, I think I'm as much like him as I care to be.

As, such is the marvelous journey of life.

I am convinced that most women could stand a heaping dose of scandalous grace that enables them to cut themselves—as well as one another—some serious slack. . . . It is this grace . . . that truly becomes "the icing on the cake" of life—freeing us as women and provoking us to live outwardly with mercy and forgiveness toward one another and ourselves.

JULIE ANN BARNHILL
Scandalous Grace

PROMISES
ABOUT PEACE AND LOVE

*Let us pursue the things which
make for peace and the
things by which one may edify another.*

ROMANS 14:19

*But the fruit of the Spirit is love,
joy, peace, longsuffering, kindness, goodness,
faithfulness, gentleness, self-control.*

GALATIANS 5:22

*He Himself is our peace,
who has made both one, and has broken down
the middle wall of division between us.*

EPHESIANS 2:14

*Walk worthy of the calling with
which you were called,
with all lowliness and gentleness.*

EPHESIANS 4:1

WHEN PEACE ABOUNDS

a Belgian poet once said that if the world is spherical, it is made that way so love and friendship and peace can go around it. I like that thought. And I've traveled enough to know there's truth to it. When we give love, it comes back to us; when we're friendly, others are friendly too; and when peace abounds, it reproduces itself. . . .

It's not just that Belgian poet who encourages us to share friendship, love, and peace, but we have been summoned by the Savior himself to do it. We are commanded to introduce people to him, train them in the way they should live under his love and protection, instruct them in his teachings. And when we do this, he has promised us his constant presence. What could be more loving and fulfilling than such a powerful assignment and such a personal promise?

LUCI SWINDOLL
Boundless Love

PROMISES
TO HELP YOU FORGIVE

*"If you forgive the sins of any,
they are forgiven them; if you retain the
sins of any, they are retained."*

JOHN 20:23

*Forgive us our debts,
as we forgive our debtors.*

MATTHEW 6:12

*"If you forgive men their trespasses,
your heavenly Father will also forgive you.
But if you do not forgive
men their trespasses, neither will your Father
forgive your trespasses."*

MATTHEW 6:13—15

Unforgiveness Is a Weed

i learned to forgive in a garden. As a child, I had an argument with my younger cousin. She told me if I didn't apologize, I couldn't come to her fifth birthday party that day. I was too proud, even at age six, to say "I'm sorry." I decided instead to miss my cousin's party.

Later that afternoon, as I sat sullenly on the sofa, hearing the birthday festivities next door, my grandmother Mama designed a teachable moment to talk with me about forgiveness. She took me to her gardens. We often talked and prayed as we walked hand-in-hand through her fragrant blooms on long summer afternoons. . . .

"Unforgiveness is like a weed in my garden," she told me as she knelt down to pull up a handful of wild plants. "Watch for them, 'Nisey. Pull 'em up as soon as they start to seed. Don't let them grow for one minute in your garden. Or they'll ruin your flower beds."

DENISE GEORGE
Cultivating a Forgiving Heart

PROMISES TO HELP YOU
KEEP IN TUNE WITH OTHERS

Comfort each other and edify one another,
just as you also are doing.
Be at peace among yourselves.

1 THESSALONIANS 5:11, 13

"I will be a Father to you,
and you shall be My sons and daughters,"
says the Lord Almighty.

2 CORINTHIANS 6:18

As each one has received a gift,
minister it to one another, as good stewards
of the manifold grace of God.

1 PETER 4:10

In Tune with Each Other

*a*n orchestra, to be worthy of its name, is like love. It demands *doing* as well as *feeling*. And it *takes practice, practice*, PRACTICE. Its members may not feel like correcting the mistakes, but they do—until the problem is resolved. They may not feel that they can endure going over and over the areas in which they continue to make mistakes, but they do—until they can communicate, share, and encourage the other members in spite of the difficulties. Only then can they become a "whole." . . .

Each instrument occupies a special "chair." Each adds a unique movement. Yet each must retain its individual beauty. And oh, how fine-tuned each instrument must be! . . .

We form an orchestra, too. Each of us is an integral part of the whole with our families, coworkers, friends. . . . To create a symphony, we must keep our ears tuned to one another, our eyes focused on the Director.

JUNE MASTERS BACHER
The Quiet Heart

PROMISES ABOUT LOVING OTHERS

Fulfill my joy be being likeminded,
having the same love,
being of one accord, of one mind.

PHILIPPIANS 2:2

Love bears all things, believes all things,
hopes all things, endures all things.

1 CORINTHIANS 13:7

Beloved, let us love one another,
for love is of God; and everyone who loves is
born of God and knows God. He who
does not love does not know God, for God is love.

1 JOHN 4:7–8

A COMMUNITY OF LOVE

a recent Zogby/Forbes ASAP poll asked respondents, What would you like most to be known for? Being intelligent? Good looking? Having a great sense of humor? A full half of respondents checked off an unexpected answer: They said they would like a reputation for "being authentic." In a world of spin and hype, the postmodern generation is searching desperately for something real and authentic. They will not take Christians seriously unless [we] demonstrate an authentic way of life. . . .

In the days of the early church, the thing that most impressed their neighbors in the Roman Empire was the community of love they witnessed among believers. "Behold how they love one another," it was said. In every age, the most persuasive evidence for the gospel is not words or arguments but a living demonstration of God's character through Christians' love for one another, expressed in both their words and their actions.

NANCY PEARCEY
Total Truth

PROMISES ABOUT GOD'S GRACE

*If we confess our sins, He is faithful and just
to forgive us our sins and
to cleanse us from all unrighteousness.*

1 JOHN 1:9

*The LORD is my shepherd; I shall not want.
He makes me to lie down in green pastures;
He leads me beside the still waters.
He restores my soul; He leads me in the paths
of righteousness for His name's sake.*

PSALM 23:1–3

*Have mercy upon me, O God, according to
Your lovingkindness; according to the multitude
of Your tender mercies, blot out my transgressions.
Wash me thoroughly from my iniquity,
and cleanse me from my sin.
For I acknowledge my transgressions. . . .
Wash me, and I shall be whiter than snow.*

PSALM 51:1–3, 7

FINDING FREEDOM
IN GOD'S GRACE

i know what it's like to have a past you'd just as soon forget. A past that you had no control over—your family of origin; your mother's choice of lifestyle; your family's battle with alcohol—as well as a past of misgivings made by your own free will. . . .

We all have "issues." We all carry burdens and regrets. And we all play a shell game of sorts, hoping to hide and deflect the broken places of our lives. But I say it's time to embrace truth.

So why not:

> Embrace the fact that you are a mess of magnificent proportions?
> Embrace the fact that you are not alone?
> Embrace the lavish reality of divine grace . . . that heals, restores, covers, forgives, renews, and abounds?

What true freedom!

JULIE ANN BARNHILL
Scandalous Grace

He will yet fill your mouth with laughing,
and your lips with rejoicing.

JOB 8:21

Then our mouth was filled with laughter,
and our tongue with singing.
Then they said among the nations,
"The LORD has done great things for them."

PSALM 126:2

A time to weep,
and a time to laugh;
a time to mourn,
and a time to dance.

ECCLESIASTES 3:4

WHY NOT HAVE SOME FUN?

*m*y grandmother never went out and purchased a new hat to combat the blahs. Money didn't grow on sassafras bushes; and, besides, she preferred a sunbonnet. But, oh yes, she had a cure. "Let's do something impulsive!" she used to say. "Let's go for a tramp in the woods. . . ."

When we'd come home we'd do an impulsive deed for a neighbor. Today, I looked back and tried to recall some of the things we did—because they're exactly what I plan to do!

1) Write a letter when it's not your turn!
2) Call somebody you haven't heard from in years;
3) Make a batch of cookies and take them to a shut-in; and
4) Go out and look for a stranger to smile at!

JUNE MASTERS BACHER
Quiet Moments for Women

PROMISES ABOUT BEING KIND

Be of one mind, live in peace;
and the God of love and peace will be with you.

2 CORINTHIANS 13:11

Walk in love, as Christ also has loved us
and given Himself for us.

EPHESIANS 5:2

Behold, how good and how pleasant it is for
brethren to dwell together in unity!

PSALM 133:1

As we have opportunity,
let us do good to all.

GALATIANS 6:10

Be Kind to Everyone

When I was three years old, my mother said something so horrible to me that I repressed it for thirty-five years. In all fairness, my mother was drunk. Desperation pulled her there. I told my counselor that my mother had said something awful to me, though I could not recall what. . . . To which my counselor calmly assured me that when it was time, I would. When I finally did recall it, I realized two things. First, in response to that painful phrase I had been driven all my life to prove her wrong and I was tired of the fight. Second, if I was going to get past this, I was going to have to be kind to myself. I didn't know how to do this. I had to ask God to teach me.

I went to my husband and a few Christian friends . . . and told them what I was going through. They prayed for me. They brought flowers and dinners. They sent cards. God helped me then. He's still helping me today. . . . I encountered a statement by John Watson during this season that's stuck: "Be kind; everyone you meet is fighting a hard battle." I believe it.

CHRISTINE WOOD
Character Witness

PROMISES ABOUT
RESPECTING OTHERS

Through love serve one another.
GALATIANS 5:13

Confess your trespasses to one another,
and pray for one another,
that you may be healed.
JAMES 5:16

[Give] thanks always
for all things to God the Father
in the name of our Lord Jesus Christ,
submitting to one another
in the fear of God.
EPHESIANS 5:20—22

RESPECT AND DIGNITY

Women were the first to be present at Jesus' birth, the last present at Jesus' crucifixion, and the first to be given the incredible privilege of sharing the great and good news of the Resurrection. Throughout his life Jesus treated women with great respect and dignity. . . .

In a day and time when the Orthodox Jew would include in his morning prayers, "I thank thee God, I am not a slave, I am not a Gentile, I am not a woman," Jesus made firm friends and followers of slaves, Gentiles, and women! . . . Women from all levels of society were involved in Christ's life and ministry. They ranked among his closest earthly friends (Mary and Martha) and assisted and traveled with him on his tours of ministry, helping to support him out of their own means (Luke 8:1–3).

Women who were sinners found forgiveness, women who were sick found health, and women who were dead found life!

JILL BRISCOE
Heartstrings

A gracious woman retains honor.

The words of a wise . . .
mouth are gracious,
but the lips of a fool shall
swallow him up.

ECCLESIASTES 10:12

As the elect of God, holy and beloved,
put on tender mercies, kindness, humility,
meekness, longsuffering.

COLOSSIANS 3:12

A Gracious Heart

*n*o sooner had I turned forty, than I started receiving catalogs promoting products guaranteed to combat the effects of aging—they promise me younger, clearer skin; fewer wrinkles; no more dark shadows; more energy; prettier nails and hair; and improved eyesight and hearing. The implication is that, as I get older, what matters most is looking and feeling younger.

However, the fact is, I am getting older, and in this fallen world, that means my body is slowly deteriorating. I look in the mirror and see lines that weren't there ten years ago; I am definitely gray-headed. . . .

But I refuse to buy into the lie that those things are ultimate tragedies or that my biological clock can somehow be reversed. I am not trying to hasten my physical decline, but neither am I going to get consumed with fighting off the inevitable. As I get older, I want to focus on those things that God says matter most—things like letting His Spirit cultivate in me a gracious, wise, kind, loving heart.

NANCY LEIGH DEMOSS
Lies Women Believe

FINDING JOY BY
MAKING WISE CHOICES

PART FOUR

*We live and survive by wisdom,
a gift that always requires us
to choose one thing
over another.*

JAN SILVIOUS

The LORD God said, "It is not good that man should be alone; I will make him a helper comparable to him." Out of the ground the LORD God formed every beast of the field and every bird of the air, and brought them to Adam to see what he would call them. And whatever Adam called each living creature, that was its name. So Adam gave names to all cattle, to the birds of the air, and to every beast of the field. But for Adam there was not found a helper comparable to him.

And the LORD God caused a deep sleep to fall on Adam, and he slept; and He took one of his ribs, and closed up the flesh in its place. Then the rib which the LORD God had taken from man He made into a woman, and He brought her to the man.

And Adam said: "This is now bone of my bones and flesh of my flesh; she shall be called Woman, because she was taken out of Man."

GENESIS 2:18–23

THE JOY OF
MAKING WISE CHOICES

i am Eve, mother of every human being. If I close my eyes I can still remember the sweetness of walking with God in the cool of the day. That was before my heart flirted with temptation; before I made a fatal error.

Adam and I knew the serpent was crafty. But I underestimated the seductive power of his voice. I thought I could handle a conversation with him. How wrong I was. Conversations require cooperation. To cooperate you must grant authority to influence.

The serpent's influence was deadly. The more I spoke with him, the more reasonable his words became. . . .

The serpent was deceptive, but I held the power of choice. I chose to converse with him. I chose to make his words an option. I chose to elevate my desires above God's will. And my choice altered human history.

All choices do.

ALICIA BRITT CHOLE
Pure Joy

PROMISES TO
HELP YOU LIVE BY FAITH

Faith is the substance of things hoped for,
the evidence of things not seen.

HEBREWS 11:1

If you have faith as a mustard seed,
you will say to this mountain,
"move from here to there," and it will move.

MATTHEW 17:20

Count it all joy when you fall
into various trials, knowing that the testing
of your faith produces patience.

JAMES 1:2

LIVING BY FAITH

i always smile when someone tells me he or she has no faith, because I know it's probably not true. Everyone lives by faith to a certain extent. When you go to a doctor, you need faith to trust his diagnosis. When the pharmacy fills your prescription, you have faith that you'll receive the appropriate medicine. When you eat at a restaurant, you trust that the people serving you have not contaminated or poisoned the food. (Some restaurants require more faith than others.) Every day is a walk of faith on some level. . . .

We choose what we will believe in. Some people choose to believe in themselves, some in government, some in evil, some in science, . . . some in God. The only person I've ever known who didn't believe in anything ended up in a mental hospital because it drove her crazy. Faith is something we can't live without.

Faith is something we can't die without either. Our faith determines what happens to us after we leave this world. If you have faith in Jesus, you know that your eternal future is secure.

STORMIE OMARTIAN
The Power of a Praying Wife

PROMISES TO HELP
YOU COPE WITH UNFAIRNESS

The LORD makes poor and makes rich;
He brings low and lifts up.

1 SAMUEL 2:7

He is not partial to princes,
nor does He regard the rich more than the poor;
for they are all the work of His hands.

JOB 34:19

In all things we commend ourselves as ministers
of God: in much patience, in tribulations,
in needs, in distresses, in stripes,
in imprisonments, in tumults, in labors,
in sleeplessness, in fastings; by purity,
by knowledge, by longsuffering, by kindness,
by the Holy Spirit, by sincere love.

2 CORINTHIANS 6:4–6

Don't Fret Over Unfairness

almost two decades ago I cohosted a radio program. At the time it was unique because two women hosted it. We had a good idea and put a lot of work into making the program a success. Unfortunately, two and a half years into the program, the two of us decided that it would be best to go our separate ways. . . .

Then three months after I left, the program was nominated for a very prestigious award. I am ashamed to admit that the envy and jealousy I felt turned . . . into big-time fretting. I was angry because I wouldn't be getting the award, and I was equally upset that my former cohost would be. . . .

Up until the night the award was given, I chewed over how unfair this was like a dog gone mad over a flea! . . . I look back on this time in my life and think, *What a waste of energy.* It changed nothing and only made me tense, irritable, and worn out.

Fretting—for whatever reason—is miserable. It makes you feel small and embittered. Not a way to be.

JAN SILVIOUS
Look at It This Way

PROMISES ABOUT
HEARING GOD'S VOICE

The counsel of the LORD stands forever;
the plans of His heart to all generations.

PSALM 33:11

Man shall not live by bread alone, but by
every word that proceeds from the mouth of God.

MATTHEW 4:4

I will delight myself
in Your commandments, which I love.

PSALM 119:47

The Voice of Our Shepherd

*t*he Eastern shepherd of Jesus' day raised his sheep primarily in the Judean uplands. The countryside was rocky, hilly, and filled with deep crevices and ravines. Patches of grass were sparse. So the shepherd had to establish a personal, working relationship with each sheep, developing its love and trust in him in order to lead it to where the path was the smoothest, the pasture was the greenest, the water was the cleanest, and the nights were the safest. The shepherd always *led* the sheep. He knew their names, and when he called them, they recognized his voice, following him like a swarm of little chicks follows the mother hen. When he stopped, the sheep huddled closely around him, pressing against his legs. Their personal relationship with him was based on his voice, which they knew and trusted.

Our Good Shepherd is Jesus, and the voice of the Good Shepherd is the Word of God. Our Shepherd speaks to us through the written words of our Bible, and His words are personal.

ANNE GRAHAM LOTZ
I Saw the Lord

PROMISES ABOUT
TAKING TIME TO REST

Come to Me, all you who labor
and are heavy laden, and I will give you rest.
MATTHEW 11:28–29

Remember the Sabbath day, to keep it holy.
EXODUS 20:8

In six days the LORD made the heavens
and the earth, the sea, and all that is in them,
and rested the seventh day. Therefore the
LORD blessed the Sabbath day and hallowed it.
EXODUS 20:11

REST AND APPRECIATE LIFE

S ome of you will appreciate my newfound area of excellence: doing nothing and resting afterward. It flies in the face of the Puritan work ethic we've all been taught and feels more decadent than a five-pound box of Godiva chocolates all to yourself. I would love to start a new habit amongst us perpetually tired women: ritualized resting.

Doesn't it seem that Sunday afternoons were specially made for napping? . . . I've always felt cheated that we live in a country that doesn't embrace the afternoon siesta. . . .

I love that the Bible tells us God didn't create Sabbath for Himself but that it was a life principle we human beings were desperately in need of. It seems that one of the most difficult things to do is to truly cease from all of our efforts and then relax and enjoy our life apart from the work of it. . . . I challenge you to start taking a day once a week to truly rest and appreciate the life God has given you.

ANITA RENFROE
The Purse-Driven Life

PROMISES TO HELP
YOU COPE WITH CRITICISM

If you are reproached for the name of Christ,
blessed are you, for the Spirit of glory
and of God rests upon you. . . . If anyone suffers
as a Christian, let him not be ashamed, but
let him glorify God in this matter.

1 PETER 4:14, 16

"Blessed are you when they revile
and persecute you, and say all kinds of evil
against you falsely for My sake.
Rejoice and be exceedingly glad, for great
is your reward in heaven, for so they persecuted
the prophets who were before you."

MATTHEW 5:11–12

In quietness and confidence
shall be your strength.

ISAIAH 30:15

COPING WITH CRITICISM

everyone who has ever walked on this earth has been criticized—even the only perfect person who ever lived. Jesus came to Earth to walk among us, to show us what the Father was like, and also to let us know He understood what it was like to live as we do, rubbing shoulders with difficult people.

No matter what Jesus did, He couldn't please the religious leaders of the day. If He healed, it was on the wrong day. If He ate dinner, it was with the wrong people. If He told the truth about Himself, He was called a liar. . . . He knows what it feels like to take it on the chin, day after day. . . .

Criticism is part of life. But just because "they said," it doesn't make it so. Remember that. And the next time "they say," take the mercy and accept the help that Jesus offers—and then keep on going. It's part of the journey.

JAN SILVIOUS
Look at It This Way

PROMISES ABOUT
KEEPING LIFE IN BALANCE

*He said to them,
"Come aside by yourselves to a deserted place
and rest a while." For there were many coming
and going, and they did not
even have time to eat.
So they departed to a deserted place
in the boat by themselves.*

MATTHEW 6:31–32

*Nothing is better for a man
than that he should eat and drink, and that
his soul should enjoy good in his labor.*

ECCLESIASTES 2:24

Be still, and know that I am God.

PSALM 46:10

KEEPING LIFE IN BALANCE

*L*et's pause a minute and enjoy the view," the guide said as the hikers stopped for breath on a nature walk at the Grand Canyon.

Everyone gasped in awe at the splendor spread below. The *huff-puff* of the steep mountain trail robbed the procession of a chance to see the cathedral-like monuments . . . time had carved along the way.

"Were those formations there when we passed?" one of the tourists teased.

The guide nodded seriously. "They were. But in our struggle to reach the top, we missed the view."

Guilty as charged. . . . Are we in such a rush to climb the ladder of success that we never look over our shoulders? So we reach the top . . . so we bump our heads on the very ceiling of achievement? How sad to realize one day that the rush to a destination robbed us of the joy of traveling.

JUNE MASTERS BACHER
The Quiet Heart

Peace I leave with you,
My peace I give to you; not as the world gives
do I give to you. Let not your
heart be troubled, neither let it be afraid.

JOHN 14:27

We do not have a High Priest who
cannot sympathize with our weaknesses,
but was in all points tempted as we are, yet
without sin. Let us therefore come boldly to the
throne of grace, that we may obtain mercy
and find grace to help in time of need.

HEBREWS 4:15-16

Therefore I take pleasure in infirmities,
in reproaches, in needs, in persecutions,
in distresses, for Christ's sake.
For when I am weak, then I am strong.

2 CORINTHIANS 12:10

GOD'S STRENGTH
FOR MY WEAKNESS

i admit that some days the weight of blindness falls heavy upon me. Sometimes even a simple thing like wearing matching socks can seem like a monumental challenge. . . . When those times come, blindness becomes an uninvited guest that stifles my dreams by turning ordinary routines into such extraordinary tasks that they leave me worn out and discouraged. On those mornings, when the list of questions is longer than the list of answers, my fatigue seems more powerful than my faith, and not even sheer grit seems enough to propel me out of bed to face the day.

So guess what I do?

Before I get up, I fall down. . . .

The *ultimate* fall is the one that happens in my heart when, with complete abandon, I yield my entire self and fall before my heavenly Father. He finds me there in my weakness and lovingly lifts me. . . . On days when I can't rise, He *carries* me.

JENNIFER ROTHSCHILD
Lessons I Learned in the Dark

PROMISES ABOUT
TAKING TIME TO PRAY

In Your presence is fullness of joy;
at Your right hand are pleasures forevermore.

PSALM 16:11

The eyes of the LORD are on the righteous,
and His ears are open to their prayers.

1 PETER 3:12

I set my face toward the Lord God
to make request by prayer and . . . I prayed to the
LORD my God, and made confession, and said,
"O Lord, great and awesome God,
who keeps His covenant and mercy with
those who love Him, and with those
who keep His commandments."

DANIEL 9:3–4

Whatever things you ask in prayer,
believing, you will receive.

MATTHEW 21:22

TAKING TIME TO PRAY

*t*imes change, but our basic needs remain stable. We need rest. You should see my neighbor. While I rush through one job with my mind on the next in line, she just drops down on the grass, idly chewing a pepperwood stem. "I'm unable to finish all that needs doing today, so what's the rush?" "I accomplish more if I sit a spell—not working—just thinking and appreciating.". . .

Somewhere there's a recipe for people like me who try to do a year's work in one day—and rob themselves of "thinking time." My friend reads "so I can know the hopes and dreams in a world before my time," she says. My friend listens to music "so I can enlarge my heart and mind." My friend prays "so I can enlarge my soul." Her philosophy is contagious.

JUNE MASTERS BACHER
Quiet Moments for Women

PROMISES ABOUT
GOD'S REDEMPTION

He has sent redemption to His people;
He has commanded His covenant forever:
Holy and awesome is His name.

PSALM 111:9

All have sinned and fall short of the glory of God,
being justified freely by His grace
through the redemption that is in Christ Jesus.

ROMANS 3:23–24

In Him we have redemption
through His blood, the forgiveness of sins,
according to the riches of His grace.

EPHESIANS 1:7

GOD REDEEMS OUR PAST

*L*ife experience has shown me this truth, which is verified by social scientists: our childhood sets the stage for how we act out the rest of our lives. What we experienced as children determines the props on the stage of our lives. In different acts of our play we can change the props. We can paint them, reupholster them or change their position in the room—but they remain onstage with us. Throughout our lives we will face problems, the roots of which go back to our childhood. . . .

Each experience we have had—regardless of how embarrassing, sad, shameful or even seemingly insignificant—has the potential to be used redemptively by God in the people whose paths cross ours. If the people who came to a Galilean hillside with their meager and simple food had refused to relinquish it to the disciples, we wouldn't have the marvelous miracle of Jesus feeding a multitude. Sometimes I imagine the people on that hillside coming to us and encouraging us by saying, "Give your stories away and get ready for God to use them beyond your wildest hopes and dreams!"

CHRISTINE WOOD
Character Witness

PROMISES ABOUT
RESPECTING YOUR HUSBAND

*Let each one of you in particular
so love his own wife as himself, and let the wife
see that she respects her husband.*

EPHESIANS 5:33 NIV

*[Let] older women . . . be reverent in behavior,
not slanderers, not given to much wine,
teachers of good things—that they admonish the
young women to love their husbands,
to love their children.*

TITUS 2:3—4

An excellent wife is the crown of her husband.

PROVERBS 12:4

*He who finds a wife finds a good thing,
and obtains favor from the LORD.*

PROVERBS 18:22

Respecting Your Husband

*g*od requires the husband to *love* his wife, but the wife is required to have *respect* for her husband. I assume no woman would marry a man she didn't love, but too often a wife loses respect for her husband after they've been married awhile. Loss of respect seems to precede loss of love and is more hurtful to a man than we realize. . . .

If this has already happened to you, and you know you've shown disrespect for your husband, confess it to God right now. Say, "Lord, I confess I do not esteem my husband the way Your Word says to. There is a wall in my heart that I know was erected as a protection against being hurt. But I am ready to let it come down so that my heart can heal.". . .

Praying like this will free you to see your man's potential for greatness as opposed to his flaws. It will enable you to say something positive that will encourage, build up, give life, and make the marriage better.

STORMIE OMARTIAN
The Power of a Praying Wife

PROMISES ABOUT
ENJOYING GOD'S CREATION

God blessed them, and God said to them,
"Be fruitful and multiply;
fill the earth and subdue it. . . .
See, I have given you every herb that yields seed
which is on the face of all the earth,
and every tree whose fruit yields seed;
to you it shall be for food."

GENESIS 1:28–29

While the earth remains,
seedtime and harvest,
cold and heat,
winter and summer,
and day and night
shall not cease.

GENESIS 8:22

The earth is the LORD's, and all its fullness,
the world and those who dwell therein.

PSALM 24:1

ENJOYING GOD'S CREATION

*t*he garden looks as rumpled as clothes left in the dryer too long. It looks at you with the same accusing eyes. Enough beans remain for tonight's vegetable dish, but in this unpredicted heatwave isn't it easier to take something from the freezer? . . . Why bother? . . . Working in the garden offers an intimate contact with God through the earth and its power for growing things. . . .

If there's one among us who has never known the thrill of growing things, try it! You have no need for a course in botany, biology or chemistry. Just read the seed catalogues, the directions on the seed packets, start digging, raking, smoothing and praying. There! Do you feel the surge of life beneath your hands! You are helping this earth (that God Himself planted in the beginning) to perpetuate life. Something happens between you and God that's very special and very intimate. Then, with the harvest, there comes a certain knowing that you have been in direct touch with the Creator. What joy!

JUNE MASTERS BACHER

Quiet Moments for Women

FINDING JOY IN A SERVANT HEART

PART FIVE

*God isn't interested
in my image;
He's concerned with
my heart.*

LUCI SWINDOLL

*James and John, the sons of Zebedee [and Salome],
came to Him, saying, "Teacher, . . . grant us that
we may sit, one on Your right hand and the other
on Your left, in Your glory."*

*But Jesus said to them, "You do not know
what you ask. Are you able to drink the cup that I
drink, and be baptized with the baptism that I
am baptized with?"*

They said to Him, "We are able."

*So Jesus said to them, "You will indeed drink
the cup that I drink, and with the baptism I am
baptized with you will be baptized; but to sit on
My right hand and on My left is not Mine to give,
but it is for those for whom it is prepared." . . .*

*Jesus . . . said to them, "You know that those
who are considered rulers over the Gentiles lord it
over them, and their great ones exercise authority
over them. Yet it shall not be so among you; but
whoever desires to become great among you shall
be your servant. . . . For even the Son of Man
did not come to be served, but to serve, and to
give His life a ransom for many."*

MARK 10:35-45

The Joy of a Servant Heart

When Jesus first asked James and John to follow him, Salome (their mother) heartily approved. After all, there was talk that Jesus was the long-awaited Messiah. Early involvement in his ministry would give her sons a leg-up in the kingdom-building process. With their motivation, abilities, and self-confidence, they could even be second and third in rank behind Jesus. . . . No only would she be the wife of Zebedee; she would be the mother of James and John, "leaders of the kingdom." . . .

Power meant a lot to James. Imagine his astonishment when Jesus said, "Whoever wants to become great among you must be your servant."

God's idea of success and our idea of success are often polar opposites. . . . James's ambitions and drives would change. His mother's would also change. In Scripture we see that Salome was at the cross (Mark 15:40–41) and at the tomb to anoint Jesus' body with spices (Mark 16:1). She, too, was walking as a servant—giving of herself even in Jesus' final moments on earth and serving him in death.

DONNA VANLIERE
They Walked with Him

Love one another,
as I have loved you.

JOHN 15:12

"Whoever desires to be first among you,
let him be your slave—just as the Son of Man
did not come to be served, but to serve, and
to give His life a ransom for many."

MATTHEW 20:27–29

[She] who is greatest among you,
let [her] be as the younger, and [she] who
governs as [she] who serves.

LUKE 22:26

SERVING OTHERS
GRACIOUSLY

brother Lawrence, a monastery cook, was sought out by the scholarly not for his sauces but for his sense, his God-sense. This monk from the order of the Carmelites Dechausses lived in the clatter of his kitchen environment with a constant ear open to heaven. Servanthood for this lumbering brother was not an effort but a pleasure, not degrading but a privilege.

I confess I prefer to be served rather than serve, especially at mealtime. The clatter in my kitchen has too often been from my grumbling as I lumber between my sink and stove. I don't find cooking easy, and seldom do I receive applause for my clumsy culinary efforts. I think servanthood must be similar in that it's unnatural for most of us and often, if our sacrifices go unnoticed, we are left stewing in our own sauce.

I wonder how many times a day I miss servant opportunities in which I could extend myself in gracious ways.

PATSY CLAIRMONT

Mending Your Heart in a Broken World

PROMISES ABOUT
SHOWING GOD'S GLORY

To the end that my glory may
sing praise to You and not be silent.
LORD my God,
I will give thanks to You forever.

PSALM 30:12

In God is my salvation and my glory;
the rock of my strength,
and my refuge, is in God.

PSALM 62:7

Not unto us, O LORD, not unto us,
but to Your name give glory,
because of Your mercy,
because of Your truth.

PSALM 115:1

GOD'S GLORY IN OUR LIVES

i have two containers for flowers. One is an old clay pot, the other is a beautiful cut-glass vase. Occasionally, I receive a lovely bouquet of roses. If I put them in the vase, the glory is shared. If I put them in the pot, attention is drawn to the blossoms. "What beautiful flowers!" exclaim my visitors, ignoring the container.

God chooses such earthen vessels that His glory may be better displayed. In fact, He has told us that He will not share His glory with another. He insists on receiving the honor due His name.

Sometimes I want to be the cut-glass vase and draw attention to myself. I have to be reminded that my sense of importance lies in the miracle of God's choosing me. He placed His roses in my vase. In this lies my value. What use is a vase without flowers?

JILL BRISCOE
Quiet Times with God

PROMISES ABOUT
LOVE IN MARRIAGE

*Above all things have
fervent love for one another.*

1 PETER 4:8

*Let love be without hypocrisy.
Abhor what is evil. Cling to what is good.
Be kindly affectionate to one another
. . . in honor giving preference to one another.*

ROMANS 12:9–10

*Who can find a virtuous wife?
For her worth is far above rubies.*

PROVERBS 31:10

*Love suffers long and is kind; love does not envy;
love does not parade itself, is not puffed up;
does not behave rudely, does not seek its own,
is not provoked, thinks no evil; does not
rejoice in iniquity, but rejoices in the truth.*

1 CORINTHIANS 13:4–6

LOVE AND MARRIAGE

*m*arriage is not something that can be improvised. You are both embarking on a long voyage, untrained, in a frail little boat headed, inevitably, for stormy waters. . . . There may be some days when you are safely anchored in the harbor, but that's not what boats are built for. They are built for sea travel.

Walter and I had a few safe harbor days, but most of the time it seemed we were out on the ocean, bailing water, pulling people from the ocean and into the boat, and trying to keep our own signals straight as husband and wife. During those times we needed our strong co-pilot, the Holy Spirit of God. And we needed the encouragement of fellow Christians who would cheer us on from their own boats nearby. . . .

Love is a decision, a judgment. It involves the intellect and the will. . . . I am reminded of a statement by Dr. Bovet: "First you choose the one you love and then you love the one you have chosen."

INGRID TROBISCH
The Hidden Strength

PROMISES ABOUT
SHOWING HOSPITALITY

"Assuredly, I say to you,
inasmuch as you did it to one of the least of these
My brethren, you did it to Me."

MATTHEW 25:40

Ointment and perfume delight the heart,
and the sweetness of a . . .
friend gives delight by hearty counsel.

PROVERBS 27:9

She also rises while it is yet night,
and provides food for her household,
and a portion for her maidservants. . . .
She extends her hand to the poor,
yes, she reaches out her hands to the needy.

PROVERBS 31:15, 20

OPENING THE DOOR
OF HOSPITALITY

*e*verything I needed to know about being hospitable I learned from Lois the first evening she invited me to dinner in her home. . . . When I arrived, she opened the door and warmly invited me in. I followed her to the kitchen where, to be frank, I expected to see the preparation of an elaborate meal. Lois's husband was a doctor and, to be perfectly honest, that raised my expectations. I saw nothing. I smelled nothing. As I began to wonder about this meal, she opened the refrigerator door and casually asked, "Let's see, what shall we have for dinner?" She wasn't kidding! Before long I had joined her search for food and her creative approach to preparation. Then we began cooking it together. Inwardly I breathed a big sigh of relief. *Even I can do this*, I thought.

After experiencing this comfortable approach, not only did I know I could do this, but my heart desired to do it. When our hospitality emphasizes pleasing people rather than elaborately preparing for them, much of the stress evaporates.

CHRISTINE WOOD
Character Witness

PROMISES TO
HELP YOU FORGIVE AND FORGET

*Not that we are sufficient of ourselves
to think of anything as being from ourselves,
but our sufficiency is from God.*

2 CORINTHIANS 3:5

*Let your gentleness be known to all men.
The Lord is at hand. Be anxious for nothing,
but in everything by prayer and supplication,
with thanksgiving, let your requests be
made known to God; and the peace of God,
which surpasses all understanding, will guard
your hearts and minds through Christ Jesus.*

PHILIPPIANS 4:5–7

The thoughts of the righteous are right.

PROVERBS 12:5

FORGIVING AND FORGETTING

*L*eftovers . . . again! How much of that dish did we make?!!! . . .

No, this is not about . . . cousin Harry's triple-fried chicken or our own energy-producing five-bean chili. This addictive leftover is the ultimate classic: Have you ever served yourself *rehash of the past?*

Somewhere, somehow, someone hurt us and we have kept that wound in our active memory, pressing rewind and play in the theatre of our minds. With each rehearsal, we see it all and feel it all and digest it all over again. . . .

Jesus tells us that this leftover is lethal: "If you do not forgive men their sins, neither will your Father forgive your sins" (Matthew 6:15). . . .

Forgiving means we stop pressing rewind and play. Forgiving means we refuse to let our minds house the moldy leftovers of other's sins against us.

ALICIA BRITT CHOLE
Sitting in God's Sunshine

PROMISES ABOUT
SERVING GOD WITH LOVE

This commandment we have from Him:
that he who loves God
must love his brother also.

1 JOHN 4:21

If anyone serves Me, let him follow Me;
and where I am,
there My servant will be also.
If anyone serves Me,
him My Father will honor.

JOHN 12:26

Since we are receiving a kingdom
which cannot be shaken, let us have grace,
by which we may serve God acceptably
with reverence and godly fear.

HEBREWS 12:28

SERVING GOD WITH LOVE

*a*re you willing to do whatever God asks of you?

I love the story about a little boy and his grandfather walking along the beach after a storm. Hundreds of starfish had washed up on the shore and the little boy was busy picking them up and throwing them back into the water. The grandfather asked the little boy why he was doing this because he could not possibly save them all. The little boy looked at the starfish in his hand and replied, "No, but I can make a difference in the life of this one." You'll never know what kind of difference you can make until you surrender your desires for your life to the perfect mission God has for you.

In order to get a clear vision of your mission, you must understand three important biblical truths. You are a new *creation* of God, who has been *chosen* by God, to fulfill a *calling* from God. God has uniquely equipped you to answer the calling of your mission.

LYSA TERKEURST
Living Life on Purpose

PROMISES ABOUT
THE COMMITMENT TO LOVE

Beloved, if God so loved us,
we also ought to love one another.

1 JOHN 4:11

We have known and believed
the love that God has for us. God is love,
and he who abides in love
abides in God, and God in him.

1 JOHN 4:16

Love never fails.
And now abide faith, hope, love, these three;
but the greatest of these is love.

12 CORINTHIANS 13:8, 13

LOVE IS A COMMITMENT

We all want to love and be loved in a way that *feels* good.

Greeting card companies make millions from our desire to somehow express a love that is different from all others, a love that is deeply committed. All of us probably have a drawer where there is a little stack of sentimental cards with words of undying love swirled across the front of each delicate offering. Yet whether they are cards that we have given and saved after the object of our love has read them, or cards that we have received, let's face it, that drawer full of cards is not what love is all about.

The major myth about love and a love relationship is that it always looks pretty and feels good. We want the objects of our love to be pretty, act pretty, and make us feel good. That is just the raw bottom line. Because of that myth, too often we are faced with the fact that real love has nothing to do with "prettiness" or "good feelings." Real love has to do with commitment and choices. It is the overarching principle in a meaningful relationship.

JAN SILVIOUS
Moving Beyond the Myths

PROMISES ABOUT GOD'S CONTROL

If God is for us, who can be against us?
He who did not spare His own Son, but delivered
Him up for us all, how shall He not with Him
also freely give us all things?

ROMANS 8:31–32

Who shall separate us from the love of Christ?
Shall tribulation, or distress, or persecution,
or famine, or nakedness, or peril, or sword? . . .
We are more than conquerors through Him
who loved us. For I am persuaded that neither
death nor life, nor angels nor principalities
nor powers, nor things present nor things to come,
nor height nor depth, nor any other
created thing, shall be able to separate us from
the love of God which is in Christ Jesus our Lord.

ROMANS 8:35–39

"My thoughts are not your thoughts,
nor are your ways My ways," says the LORD.

ISAIAH 55:8

God's in Complete Control

Shortly after my son's divorce, I realized that I had drawn a blueprint for my life that included plans for each member of my family. I loved that blueprint and protected it fiercely. When the flames of reality consumed it, I was devastated. After crying gallons of bitter tears and praying for many hours, I knew I had to submit to the sovereignty of God. I had to accept His right as my Creator to do whatever He wills with me, even if it included allowing this crushing heartbreak. . . .

As a visual demonstration of the exercise of submission . . . and a statement of trust in God's goodness, I took a piece of notebook paper from my journal and at the top of the page I wrote the words: *My Agenda*. Under that heading, I listed all of the dreams and wishes (expectations) I harbored for myself and for the ones I loved. Then I stood over a trash can and tore the paper into a hundred tiny pieces. . . .

I had to remind myself clearly: God is sovereign and in complete control. . . . While His doings are often beyond my understanding, the volume of His love for me is beyond all measuring.

JAN WINEBRENNER
Intimate Faith

FINDING JOY IN COMMITMENT TO CHRIST

PART SIX

You are God's priceless gift of love to His Son!

ANNE GRAHAM LOTZ

Certain women who had been healed of evil spirits and infirmities—Mary called Magdalene, out of whom had come seven demons, and Joanna the wife of Chuza, Herod's steward, and Susanna, and many others who provided for Him from their substance.

Mary stood outside by the tomb weeping, and . . . she saw two angels in white sitting, one at the head and the other at the feet, where the body of Jesus had lain. Then they said to her, "Woman, why are you weeping?" She said to them, "Because they have taken away my Lord, and I do not know where they have laid Him."

Now when she had said this, she turned around and saw Jesus standing there, and did not know that it was Jesus. Jesus said to her, "Woman, why are you weeping? Whom are you seeking?"

She, supposing Him to be the gardener, said to Him, "Sir, if You have carried Him away, tell me where You have laid Him, and I will take Him away."

Jesus said to her, "Mary!"

She turned and said to Him, "Rabboni!"

LUKE 8:2–3; JOHN 20:11–16

THE JOY OF BEING COMMITTED TO CHRIST

*m*ary Magdalene must be one of the most loved women of the Bible, yet she is probably one of the most misunderstood. . . . Contrary to popular belief, Mary is not the same woman as the sinner woman we read about in Luke 7. There is no evidence that she was a prostitute. There are many reasons why such a tradition has grown up around Mary, but once the subject is investigated it is plain to see that she was a prominent, wealthy woman who was healed by Christ of terrible infirmities and who is named among the women of good reputation and means, who ministered to Christ from their substance (Luke 8:1–3). . . .

She served her Lord well in life . . . and also served Him well in death. He who valued her love so dearly bequeathed to Mary one of heaven's richest honors. She was to be the first to witness Him after His resurrection and the first to be commissioned to run and tell what she had seen and heard.

JILL BRISCOE

Women in the Life of Jesus

PROMISES ABOUT
BEING FAITHFUL TO GOD

May the LORD repay every man
for his righteousness and his faithfulness.

1 SAMUEL 26:23

My eyes shall be on the faithful of the land,
that they may dwell with me; he who walks in a
perfect way, he shall serve me.

PSALM 101:6

His lord said to him,
"Well done, good and faithful servant;
you were faithful over a few things,
I will make you ruler over many things.
Enter into the joy of your lord."

MATTHEW 25:21

FAITHFUL TO USE OUR GIFTS

*a*bout a year ago we had a second phone line installed in our home that was only one digit off from the long distance information line in a certain region of South Carolina. At first I was so frustrated with the influx of callers wanting phone numbers to Bud's Seafood and Bessie's Best Bathing Suit Shop. Just as I was about to call the phone company and demand they fix the problem immediately, God reminded me of my commitment to make the most of every evangelism opportunity He gives me.

So the "God line" was born. I started proudly answering the phone, "God-line information. We don't have all the answers but we know the One who does. How may I help you?" Most of the time I get a bewildered "Huh?" on the other line, but every now and then God uses this wrong number to set divine appointments with Him.

LYSA TERKEURST
Living Life on Purpose

PROMISES ABOUT
LIVING BY FAITH

*Whatever is born of God overcomes the world.
And this is the victory that
has overcome the world—our faith.*

1 JOHN 5:4

*Without faith it is impossible to please Him,
for he who comes to God must
believe that He is, and that He is a rewarder
of those who diligently seek Him.*

HEBREWS 11:6

*Let us lay aside every weight,
and the sin which so easily ensnares us,
and let us run with endurance the race that is
set before us, looking unto Jesus,
the author and finisher of our faith,
who for the joy that was set before Him endured
the cross, despising the shame, and has
sat down at the right hand of the throne of God.*

HEBREWS 12:1–2

FAITH IN EVERYDAY LIVING

Ours is not a culture that enjoys mystery, except in a movie or a novel. And then we aren't really happy unless the mystery is solved to our satisfaction. The fact is, we don't mind not knowing if it is only for the first eighty-five minutes of a ninety-minute feature film, or for the time it takes to read . . . a Mary Higgins Clark best-seller. But as soon as final events tick down in the story, we want certainty. . . .

Such is the strength of our culture. We thrive on the tenacity of medical researchers who resist the unknown with every atom of their beings. We build laboratories and think tanks and hire people to examine mysteries and solve them for us. Yet this, what is our very strength as a society, is the fatal flaw of the life of faith.

Faith accepts that there are mysteries that will never be unraveled by the human mind. It accepts that God is transcendent; that much of what occurs on this planet will defy human explanations. It gives up the urgent, human craving to have all the answers, all the time.

JAN WINEBRENNER
Intimate Faith

PROMISES ABOUT
MANAGING YOUR TIME

My help comes from the LORD,
who made heaven and earth.

PSALM 121:1

It is good that one should hope and
wait quietly for the salvation of the LORD.

LAMENTATIONS 3:26

His divine power has given to us
all things that pertain to life and godliness.

2 PETER 1:3

He changes the times and the seasons; . . .
He gives . . . knowledge
to those who have understanding.

DANIEL 2:21

LET GOD MANAGE YOUR TIME

Yesterday I was talking to an overwhelmed friend via e-mail. She told me how her life was spinning out of control as she served on several different committees at her children's school, . . . sang in the choir, taught Sunday school, participated on the pastor search committee, . . . and so forth. The previous week, she had been out of the house every single night.

"Cynthia," I wrote, "I want you to write down everything you've done over the past two months. Then take that list and go into your prayer closet and pray. Ask God to show you what items on your list someone else could have done. Yes, I know, another person may not have done it as well as you, but that's OK. Place a mark on the list by things that only you could have done." . . .

Women today are too busy being busy. And much of what we do has no eternal value. Setting priorities and sticking to them requires much time in prayer asking God what He wants you to do and when He wants you to do it.

SHARON JAYNES AND LYSA TERKUERST
A Woman's Secret to a Balanced Life

PROMISES ABOUT
LIVING COURAGEOUSLY

Be strong and of good courage,
do not fear nor be afraid of them; for the LORD
your God, He is the One who goes with you.
He will not leave you nor forsake you.

DEUTERONOMY 31:6

Wait on the LORD; be of good courage,
and He shall strengthen your heart;
wait, I say, on the LORD!

PSALM 27:14

In God I have put my trust;
I will not be afraid.
What can man do to me?

PSALM 56:11

LIVING COURAGEOUSLY

C ome," Jesus says with a smile.

Foolhardy and daring, Peter pushes the other disciples aside and clumsily bounds over the side of the boat. Remarkably, it is as if a solid path of earth has formed beneath his feet. . . .

Like Peter, sometimes your faith takes you into uncharted or maybe even dangerous waters. Perhaps you move to another state. You have children. You take a new job. You face an empty nest. You experience life as a single parent. As long as you keep your eyes focused on Christ, you're able to keep your head above water. But then . . . *boom!* An unbridled wave capsizes your little boat of faith and drags you under. . . .

Life will beat us. It will leave us broken and gasping for air. . . . But God has promised, "I will never leave you nor forsake you" (Joshua 1:5). Dark clouds may hide Him from our sight, but He's always standing right in front of us with outstretched hands saying, "Come."

DONNA VANLIERE
They Walked with Him

*"You are the salt of the earth;
but if the salt loses its flavor, how shall it
be seasoned? It is then good for nothing
but to be thrown out and trampled underfoot
by men. You are the light of the world.
A city that is set on a hill cannot be hidden."*

MATTHEW 5:13–14

*Let your speech always be with grace,
seasoned with salt, that you may
know how you ought to answer each one.*

COLOSSIANS 4:6

*No spring yields both salt water and fresh.
Who is wise and understanding among you?
Let him show by good conduct that
his works are done in the meekness of wisdom.*

JAMES 3:12–13

Infusing Godly Values into Life

*L*ast night, I telephoned the family farm back in Maryland to see how my sister Jay was doing. She was up to her elbows in pickles! Cucumbers are ripe off the vine from Jay's garden so she's spending her evenings boiling and blanching, straining and sealing. I love my sister's pickles, and I think her secret is . . . salt. She adds a lot of salt and tells me that it's the best way to preserve a pickle at its crunchiest, tastiest best.

Those words go well together—salt and preserve. As Christians, we act as a salty preservative in this world, infusing godly values into a life around us. We have the work of restraining evil and advancing good. And just as salt brings out flavor in food, we can "season to taste" our words when the world asks us the reason for the hope that is within us.

JONI EARECKSON TADA
Diamonds in the Dust

PROMISES ABOUT
STEADFAST PRAISE

My heart is steadfast, O God,
my heart is steadfast;
I will sing and give praise.

PSALM 57:7

I will sing praise to Your name forever.

PSALM 61:8

In everything give thanks;
for this is the will of God in Christ Jesus for you.

1 THESSALONIANS 5:18

STEADFAST PRAISE

O n his second missionary journey, Paul along with Silas had several "waits" before they were led by the Spirit—in a very roundabout way—to go to Philippi. . . . I wonder what his expectations were. A city-wide evangelistic crusade? Media coverage? An equipping seminar for local pastors? . . .

We would no doubt be safe in assuming there were some *disappointments* upon arrival. Instead of an impressive crowd . . . they met a handful of women by a river and shared their faith. Then a slave girl followed them. Paul cast a demon out of her in Jesus' name, . . . and the rest is history. Paul and Silas were jailed, stripped, and severely beaten, with their feet fastened in stocks.

If I had been there, my deepest longing would have been to escape and leave! Not Paul. His longing was a deep yearning to preach the gospel and lead people to Jesus Christ. . . . Thus, his action of praying and singing hymns to God in the middle of his imprisonment led to another holy action. Instead of escaping after the earthquake, he stayed and led the jailer to Christ.

CAROL KENT

Secret Longings of the Heart

PROMISES ABOUT
STUDYING GOD'S WAYS

Teach me Your way, O LORD;
I will walk in Your truth;
unite my heart to fear Your name.

PSALM 86:11

As for God, His way is perfect;
the word of the LORD is proven;
He is a shield to all who trust in Him.

PSALM 18:30

Show me Your ways, O LORD;
teach me Your paths.

PSALM 25:4

STUDYING GOD'S WAYS

*a*s a child, my favorite part about visiting the beach was going to the boardwalk. After a day in the ocean, we'd shower, dress, and run up to the boardwalk for ice cream cones. My sisters and I would sit on a bench, lick our cones, and watch all the people stroll by. Kids with cotton candy. Lovers ambling arm-in-arm. Older ladies in flowered dresses with parasols. People-watching was the neatest part.

I still enjoy looking at people, thinking about where they live, wondering where they work, and if they're happy. Studying people, for me, is a habit.

Wouldn't it be great if we were as conscious about studying God as we were people? Watching Him, wondering about Him, looking closely at what makes Him who He is, and just . . . enjoying Him.

JONI EARECKSON TADA

Diamonds in the Dust

PROMISES ABOUT
MAKING RIGHT CHOICES

*Blessed are those servants whom the master,
when he comes, will find watching.
Assuredly, I say to you that he will gird
himself and have them sit down to eat,
and will come and serve them.*

LUKE 12:37

*I have set before you life and death,
blessing and cursing; therefore choose life,
that both you and your descendants may live.*

DEUTERONOMY 30:19

*No one can serve two masters;
for either he will hate the one and love the other,
or else he will be loyal to the one
and despise the other.
You cannot serve God and mammon.*

MATTHEW 6:24

MAKING THE RIGHT CHOICES

*t*he other day, I was driving down a busy road when I came upon a traffic light that was both green and red at the same time. I slowed, unsure of what I should do, as did the other cars coming from all directions. It was confusing and dangerous. Some people stopped, others ran right through the light, and still others pulled off to the side of the intersection.

I finally made it through the intersection and thought about this unusual happening. It was as if God were showing me a visual picture of what it's like when a person is indecisive in her obedience to Him. We can't seek to follow God wholeheartedly if part of our heart is being pulled in a different direction. We can't pursue the radically obedient life and still continue to flirt with disobedience in certain areas of our life. We can't be both red and green toward God at the same time. It gets us nowhere. It's confusing. It's dangerous.

LYSA TERKEURST
Radically Obedient, Radically Blessed

Blessed is the [woman]
who walks not in the counsel of the ungodly,
Nor stands in the path of sinners,
nor sits in the seat of the scornful;
but [her] delight is in the law of the LORD,
and in His law [she] meditates day and night.
[She] shall be like a tree
planted by the rivers of water,
that brings forth its fruit in its season,
whose leaf also shall not wither;
and whatever [she] does shall prosper.

PSALM 1:1–3

He makes me to lie down in green pastures;
He leads me beside the still waters.
He restores my soul;
He leads me in the paths of righteousness
for His name's sake.

PSALM 23:2–3

LIVING STEADFASTLY FOR CHRIST

a friend of mine recently climbed to the top of Mount Rainier for the first time. He said that the important thing in such a long climb was for the team to keep moving up, slowly but surely. . . .

My friend told me after his return from Mount Rainier of the exhilaration of reaching the top, even in a blizzard, and of being hardly able to realize that he had actually made it. It was very disappointing, then that because of the storm, his team had to come back down immediately. The hope of our walk as Christians is that we are also moving toward the top. We are on our way to meeting [God] there, face to face. But when we arrive, we won't ever have to come back down. Now it is our purpose to keep on walking and not to faint.

MARVA DAWN
To Walk and Not Faint

PROMISES ABOUT
RESTING ON THE SABBATH

*God blessed the seventh day and sanctified it,
because in it He rested from all His work
which God had created and made.*

GENESIS 2:3

*I will take My rest, and I will look from
My dwelling place like clear heat in sunshine,
like a cloud of dew in the heat of harvest.*

ISAIAH 18:4

*The LORD your God commanded you
to keep the Sabbath day.*

DEUTERONOMY 5:15

Resting on the Sabbath

So the week has been overwhelming? You want a sanitized house. Your family deserves nutritious meals. Your job is demanding (whether you are an office slave or a household servant!). You would like to take an art course, write a poem, create a garden, maybe take a trip. . . .

"I can't do it all!" you screamed above the hiss of the shower over and over when you were alone half a blissful moment.

Of course, you can't. Don't you think God knew that? That's why He created Sundays. Now the helter-skelter existence will commence anew on Monday. But maybe you can face life a day at a time if you use Sunday wisely—breathing in God in big, big doses.

JUNE MASTERS BACHER
The Quiet Heart

Finding Joy in God's Provisions

PART SEVEN

God is with us
no matter what future
we wake up in.
LESLIE WILLIAMS

Now a certain woman had a flow of blood for twelve years, and had suffered many things from many physicians. She had spent all that she had and was no better, but rather grew worse. When she heard about Jesus, she came behind Him in the crowd and touched His garment. For she said, "If only I may touch His clothes, I shall be made well."

Immediately the fountain of her blood was dried up, and she felt in her body that she was healed of the affliction. And Jesus, immediately knowing in Himself that power had gone out of Him, turned around in the crowd and said, "Who touched My clothes?"

But His disciples said to Him, "You see the multitude thronging You, and You say, 'Who touched Me?'"

And He looked around to see her who had done this thing. But the woman, fearing and trembling, knowing what had happened to her, came and fell down before Him and told Him the whole truth. And He said to her, "Daughter, your faith has made you well. Go in peace, and be healed of your affliction."

MARK 5:25–34

The Joy of God's Provisions

a certain woman in Scripture is particularly interesting to me. . . . She was known as the bleeding woman. That twelve-year hemorrhage defined who she was. . . .

The woman had tried the conventional route to deal with her problem . . . but she was not going to be healed by the physicians. . . . This Gentile woman came to a point where she was willing to do something radical and scary. She would look for and she would find Jesus. If she could just get to Him surely she could be healed. She got only close enough to Him to touch the hem of His garment, but she was healed. . . .

If you are needy in any way, you need Jesus. Moreover, He is involved in everything that involves you. I think the point to be made here is that there is always the conventional way to do things, but that doesn't always work. It is what you try first, but when there are no answers, you can get radical—look for Jesus.

JAN SILVIOUS

Moving Beyond the Myths

PROMISES ABOUT
GOD'S ANSWERS TO PRAYER

Let my prayer be set before You
as incense, the lifting up of my hands
as the evening sacrifice.

PSALM 141:2

O You who hear prayer,
to You all flesh will come.

PSALM 65:2

So I tell you,
whatever you pray for and ask,
believe that you have got it
and you shall have it.

MARK 11:24

GOD ANSWERS PRAYER

i love ordering things from clothes catalogs. The order forms . . . are like crossword puzzles— but with all the answers provided. I feel really great, clever, and all that because I can fill them in!

The order is mailed and forgotten in the rush of more immediate things. Then *bang*, right in the middle of some activity totally unrelated to my catalog order, the parcel is delivered!

How like God. The specifics of my order are carefully tabulated and delivered in his time and with eternal efficiency. The answers are sent to prayers I prayed months, even years, ago—long after I have forgotten my requests. Sometimes it no longer really matters to me if the parcel even arrives! But my words are not allowed to fall to the ground. Angels catch them and register the demand. How good of God.

JILL BRISCOE
Quiet Times with God

PROMISES ABOUT GOD'S PURPOSES

And we know that all things
work together for good to those who love God,
to those who are the called
according to His purpose.

ROMANS 8:28

Job answered the LORD and said:
"I know that You can do everything, and that
no purpose of Yours can be withheld from You."

JOB 42:1–2

The LORD of hosts has sworn, saying,
"Surely, as I have thought,
so it shall come to pass,
and as I have purposed,
so it shall stand."

ISAIAH 14:24

The LORD of hosts has purposed,
and who will annul it? His hand is stretched out,
and who will turn it back?

ISAIAH 14:27

GOD'S PURPOSES
AND INTENTIONS

You ought to see how many half-finished drawings and paintings I have in my art studio. They are piled everywhere. I get an idea, render a few quick sketches, and then my attention gets diverted—perhaps a different art project was overdue or I was up against some other deadline. Occasionally, I get back to those sketches but, more than likely, they get thrown onto a pile in the corner.

Half-finished pastels. Almost-completed paintings. Not-quite-done watercolors. I have an idea I'll never place any of them back up on my art easel.

I am so relieved my Creator doesn't approach things as I do. God always finishes what He begins. He completes every purpose. He fulfills every intention. God has a long way to go in my life, and I'm grateful that He hasn't finished with me yet.

JONI EARECKSON TADA

Diamonds in the Dust

PROMISES ABOUT
ACCEPTING WHAT GOD GIVES

*Every good gift and every perfect gift
is from above, and comes down from the Father
of lights, with whom there is
no variation or shadow of turning.*

JAMES 1:17

*By grace you have been saved through faith,
and that not of yourselves; it is the gift of God.*

EPHESIANS 2:8

*But to each one of us grace was given
according to the measure of Christ's gift.*

EPHESIANS 4:7

*If you then, being evil, know how
to give good gifts to your children, how much
more will your Father who is in heaven give good
things to those who ask Him!*

MATTHEW 7:11

ACCEPTING WHAT GOD GIVES

*f*or my birthday one year, my mother sent me a package wrapped in plain brown paper. When I opened it, there was a gaudy, multicolored Mexican straw basket inside, stuffed with tissue paper. . . . I tossed out the tissue paper, wondered what in the world I was going to do with the basket, then called to thank her for her "gift." Mother laughed when I thanked her for the basket then asked what I thought about what was inside it. I told her that nothing was inside except tissue paper, and I had thrown that out. She responded urgently, "Oh no, Anne! Inside that tissue paper is your real birthday gift!"

I ran outside, opened up the trash can, and went through the garbage piece by piece until I came up with the wad of tissue paper. Inside was a small gold ring with a lapis lazuli stone . . . from the British Museum! . . .

Sometimes God wraps His glory in hard circumstances or ugly obstacles or painful difficulties, and it just never occurs to us that within those life-shaking events is a fresh revelation of Him.

ANNE GRAHAM LOTZ
I Saw the Lord

PROMISES ABOUT
HOW TO HANDLE CRISES

Rejoice in the Lord always.
Again I will say, rejoice.

PHILIPPIANS 4:4

Be anxious for nothing, but in everything
by prayer and supplication, with thanksgiving,
let your requests be made known to God;
and the peace of God, which surpasses
all understanding, will guard your
hearts and minds through Christ Jesus.

PHILIPPIANS 4:6−7

I have learned in whatever state I am,
to be content: I know how to be abased, and I
know how to abound. Everywhere and in
all things I have learned both to be full and to be
hungry, both to abound and to suffer need.

PHILIPPIANS 4:11−12

Handling Crises God's Way

*t*he apostle Paul exhorts us (Phil. 4:6, Amplified) to pray about everything, to pour our hearts out to the Heavenly Father with "definite requests."

My problem is that having done this, having laid my concern before the Father, I get the feeling that if I do not frequently return to it in my mind and keep "worrying" it, much as a dog would a bone, then there certainly can be no chance of solving it. . . .

God seems to point out chapter four in Philippians as a blueprint for handling crises His way:

Rejoice in the Lord always.

Do not fret about anything.

Pray about everything.

Be content with our earthly lot, whatever it is.

Guard our thoughts; think only positive things.

CATHERINE MARSHALL
A Closer Walk

He who dwells in the secret place of the Most High
shall abide under the shadow of the Almighty.
I will say of the LORD,
"He is my refuge and my fortress;
my God, in Him I will trust."

PSALM 91:1—2

The LORD also will be a refuge for the oppressed,
a refuge in times of trouble.

PSALM 9:9

In the shadow of Your wings
I will make my refuge,
until these calamities have passed by.

PSALM 57:1

GOD IS OUR REFUGE

i once had an accident in my hometown. The police helped me and took me away by car. Whenever a policeman in Holland does anything, a report has to be submitted. So out came his notebook and he asked my name. "Corrie ten Boom." He looked up in surprise and asked, "Are you a member of the Ten Boom family we arrested during the way?" "Yes, I am." During that time many good policemen were forced to work for the German Gestapo; they stayed in their positions to help political prisoners. The man said, "I'll never forget that night. I was on duty when the whole Ten Boom family and about forty friends were arrested because they had helped Jews. There was an atmosphere of celebration in our police station rather than a gathering of prisoners likely to die in prison and concentration camps. I often still tell of how your father took out his Bible and read Psalm 91 and then prayed so calmly."

Ten years later the policeman still remembered which psalm my father had read: "He is my refuge and my fortress" (Psalm 91:1–2 NIV).

CORRIE TEN BOOM
Messages of God's Abundance

PROMISES ABOUT GOD'S POWER

He rules by His power forever; . . .
Oh, bless our God, you peoples!

PSALM 66:7–8

Be exalted, O LORD, in Your own strength!
We will sing and praise Your power.

PSALM 21:13

He has made the earth by His power;
He has established the world by His wisdom, and
stretched out the heaven by His understanding.

JEREMIAH 51:15

"Not by might nor by power, but by My Spirit,"
says the LORD of hosts.

ZECHARIAH 4:6

God's Power for Us

a man from Australia bought a Rolls Royce in England and took it home with him. However, he neglected to find out the horsepower. He wrote to the manufacturer but received only the terse British reply, "Adequate!" The British firm believed that was all the owner of the car needed to know.

We don't need to know how God's power works; we only need to know that His power in us is available and wholly "adequate." Use it to its full advantage for God's kingdom!

JILL BRISCOE
Quiet Times with God

*"I am the God of your father Abraham;
do not fear, for I am with you."*

GENESIS 26:24

*"Fear not, for I am with you;
be not dismayed, for I am your God.
I will strengthen you, Yes, I will help you, I will
uphold you with My righteous right hand."*

ISAIAH 41:10

*"I will dwell in them and walk among them.
I will be their God,
and they shall be My people."*

2 CORINTHIANS 6:16

God's Presence

*e*very day we witness miracles that we know no human could perform—miracles like being able to breathe, walk, talk, move, see, think, taste, and touch. Evidence of God's presence and power is all around us in the universe—the sun, the stars, the birth of each new day. And yet, like Jesus' disciples of old, we continue to search for peace outside of Him, even when He is with us moment by moment on our journey. We sometimes ask the same question the disciples did: "Who is this?" (Mark 4:41).

Well, let's unwrap the gift He is to us.

He's someone we can pray to.

He knows what we need before we ask.

He keeps His promises.

He's our example.

He understands our tears.

He's always near.

THELMA WELLS
Extravagant Grace

*Who has measured the waters
in the hollow of His hand, measured heaven
with a span and calculated
the dust of the earth in a measure?*

ISAIAH 40:12

*Unto us a Child is born,
unto us a Son is given; and the government
will be upon His shoulder. And His name will be
called Wonderful, Counselor, Mighty God,
Everlasting Father, Prince of Peace.*

ISAIAH 9:6

*Great is our Lord, and mighty in power;
His understanding is infinite.*

PSALM 147:5

*He gives power to the weak, and to
those who have no might He increases strength.*

ISAIAH 40:29

God's Might

first, imagine all the raindrops in the world. Then add all the snowflakes and hailstones, the fog and mists. Next, bring in all the creeks and ponds and puddles. Finally, add all the glaciers and snow packs, the streams and rivers, the wells and underground springs, and even all the lakes and the mammoth oceans. All the waters of the earth, added together—and God holds them in a single handful! Inconceivable!

Even if we limited our picture to just one of these bodies of water . . . the image is mind boggling. . . .

We can't even begin to imagine what God is like: all our pictures are shockingly dazzling, and yet they don't even scratch the surface of the unutterable wonder of His inexpressible infinity. Why are we such blind fools in our presumptions that we do not trust this God who exercises His might on our behalf?

MARVA DAWN
To Walk and Not Faint

Help us, O God of our salvation
for the glory of Your name; and deliver us,
and provide atonement for our sins,
for Your name's sake!

PSALM 79:9

Who provides food for the raven,
when its young ones cry to God,
and wander about for lack of food?

JOB 38:41

May He who supplies seed to the sower,
and bread for food, supply and
multiply the seed you have sown and increase
the fruits of your righteousness.

2 CORINTHIANS 9:10

GOD PROVIDES

What can people actually do to us?

They can stain our reputations, but God fully knows all hearts. They can stand in the way of opportunity, but God opens doors that no man can close. They can steal our earthly goods, but God is our true treasure. They can restrict our physical freedom, but God's Spirit is unchained. They can hinder or take our jobs, but God is our Provider. They can even kill our body, but they cannot touch our souls.

So the next time we feel threatened by someone's words or ways, let us resist the fear of people by remembering these two truths:

1. The person that stands before us is human.
2. The One that stands behind us is God.

ALICIA BRITT CHOLE
Sitting in God's Sunshine

PROMISES ABOUT
THE HOPE OF HEAVEN

Do not rejoice in this,
that the spirits are subject to you,
but rather rejoice because
your names are written in heaven.

LUKE 10:20

Blessed be the God and Father of
our Lord Jesus Christ, who according to His
abundant mercy has begotten us again to a living
hope through the resurrection of Jesus Christ
from the dead, to an inheritance incorruptible and
undefiled and that does not fade away,
reserved in heaven for you.

1 PETER 1:3–4

He who overcomes, I will make him a pillar
in the temple of My God, and he shall
go out no more. I will write on him the name of
My God and the name of the city of My God,
the New Jerusalem, which comes down
out of heaven from My God.

REVELATION 3:12

THE HOPE OF HEAVEN

i know a place where there will be no more wars.
I know a place where there will never be
another broken heart. . . .

I know a place where all our longings, all our
desires, our all will be fulfilled and found in The
One. . . .

If you asked me why I believe in God, in Jesus,
and in the hope of a place called Heaven, it would
be for this reason alone: God always wraps up what
He started. From Adam and Eve to that final tear
wiped from its beloved owner's face, God wraps up
what He started. . . .

Can you imagine what it will be like to see the
face of The One who has lavished us with His
grace, rescued us with His Cross, and purposed us
to live forever and forever with Him?

JULIE ANN BARNHILL
Exquisite Hope

*Yours, O LORD, is the greatness,
the power and the glory, the victory and the
majesty; for all that is in heaven and
in earth is Yours; Yours is the kingdom, O LORD,
and You are exalted as head over all.*

1 CHRONICLES 29:11

*How shall we escape if we neglect so great a
salvation, which at the first began to be
spoken by the Lord, and was confirmed to us by
those who heard Him, God also bearing
witness both with signs and wonders,
with various miracles, and gifts of the Holy Spirit,
according to His own will?*

HEBREWS 2:3–5

*Therefore He who supplies the Spirit to you
and works miracles among you,
does He do it by the works of the law,
or by the hearing of faith?*

GALATIANS 3:5

OUR MIRACLE-WORKING GOD

*f*or many years I believed that miracles were extraordinary events that happened only rarely as special manifestations of God's presence. The ultimate, "occasional" sign of God's blessing would be a "miraculous" healing. Jesus, of course, was known for His miracles. Many people followed Him around, hoping for a miracle sighting. I sometimes feel that those early followers were like those of us who gather to watch fireworks displays—setting up in places where we can get the best view, craning our necks upward, voting with our "oohs" and "aahs" as to the superiority of each burst and shower of light.

I believe that Jesus Himself didn't view a miracle as "a miracle" per se, but simply as another manifestation of God's love and provision for human needs. Do you think He ever doubted that He could turn water into wine? Feed the five thousand with a few loaves and fishes? Raise Lazarus? Have the donkey waiting for Him just outside Jerusalem? Jesus never doubted because He knew God would provide.

LAURIE BETH JONES
Jesus in Blue Jeans

PROMISES ABOUT GOD'S ANGELS

He shall give His angels charge over you,
to keep you in all your ways.

PSALM 91:11

Bless the LORD, you His angels,
who excel in strength, who do His word,
heeding the voice of His word.

PSALM 103:20

The Son of Man will come in the glory
of His Father with His angels, and then He will
reward each according to his works.

MATTHEW 16:27

God's Angels

*a*ngels have become too much a New Age fad these days—and the tendency is to believe that they exist only for our personal benefit. In contrast, the Bible does name angels, archangels, seraphim, and cherubim as part of the heavenly hosts and invites us to be grateful for their ministering work, including their constant war with the "spiritual forces of evil."

One favorite story summarizes all we need to know about angels anyway. When Elisha is in danger of losing his life, his awed servant panics because he can see only the horses and chariots of the Aramean army surrounding the city of Dothan (2 Kings 6:8–23). When he cries to Elisha, the prophet calmly answers, "Those who are with us are more than those who are with them," and then prays for Yahweh to open the servant's eyes . . . to see "the hills full of horses and chariots of fire."

Our problem is that we don't usually see them either. We need the Lord to open our eyes to recognize His messengers. . . . We need to take angels seriously as the forces that God constantly provides to take care of us.

MARVA DAWN
Morning by Morning

FINDING JOY
IN OBEYING GOD'S WILL

PART EIGHT

God will give us the very best
if we trust Him.
ELISABETH ELLIOT

Now in the sixth month the angel Gabriel was sent by God to a city of Galilee named Nazareth, to a virgin betrothed to a man whose name was Joseph, of the house of David. The virgin's name was Mary. And having come in, the angel said to her, "Rejoice, highly favored one, the Lord is with you; blessed are you among women!"

But when she saw him, she was troubled at his saying, and considered what manner of greeting this was. Then the angel said to her, "Do not be afraid, Mary, for you have found favor with God. And behold, you will conceive in your womb and bring forth a Son, and shall call His name JESUS.". . .

Then Mary said to the angel, "How can this be, since I do not know a man?"

And the angel answered and said to her, "The Holy Spirit will come upon you, and the power of the Highest will overshadow you; therefore, also, that Holy One who is to be born will be called the Son of God. . . ."

Then Mary said, "Behold the maidservant of the Lord! Let it be to me according to your word." And the angel departed from her.

LUKE 1:26–38

THE JOY OF
OBEYING GOD'S WILL

*m*ary was not a feeble girl, weak and without spunk, imagination, or initiative. Subsequent action proves that. But she was meek. Never confuse weak with meek. She was meek as Moses was meek—strong enough and holy enough to recognize her place under God. Thoughts of what people would say, what Joseph her fiancé would say, or how she would ever convince them that she had not been unfaithful were instantly set aside. "Here I am, the Lord's handmaid," she said. "I will accept whatever He gives me." . . .

The angel left her, the account says. Back he flies, past Mars, Jupiter, Saturn, Uranus, beyond the Southern Cross and the Milky Way. . . .

Gabriel, too, had obeyed. He delivered the message. He brought back a message: on that planet, in Galilee, in a town called Nazareth, in the house to which God had sent him, the girl named Mary had said yes.

ELISABETH ELLIOT
On Asking God Why

I have taught you in the way of wisdom;
I have led you in right paths.

PROVERBS 4:11

Your word is a lamp to my feet
and a light to my path.

PSALM 119:105

Ponder the path of your feet,
and let all your ways be established.

PROVERBS 4:26

A man's heart plans his way,
but the LORD directs his steps.

PROVERBS 16:9

FOLLOWING GOD EACH DAY

i once saw a bumper sticker that said "God is my co-pilot." That sounds spiritual, but it isn't true. The truth is that on our faith journey, God is the Pilot, and we must follow, not co-lead.

We are not in charge of the journey. We are called to restfully follow. Our Pilot is completely trustworthy. There's no need for us to fret, for He is capable of navigating us through all the turbulence of the journey. We can rest in the very situation where He has lovingly placed us. And when we do, we'll find the fabulous freedom of following.

JENNIFER ROTHSCHILD
Lessons I Learned in the Dark

PROMISES ABOUT
ACCEPTING GOD'S FORGIVENESS

Create in me a clean heart, O God,
and renew a steadfast spirit within me.

PSALM 51:10

You have forgiven the iniquity of Your people;
You have covered all their sin.

PSALM 85:2

As far as the east is from the west,
so far has He removed our transgressions from us.

PSALM 103:12

In Him we have redemption through His blood,
the forgiveness of sins,
according to the riches of His grace.

EPHESIANS 1:7

ACCEPTING GOD'S FORGIVENESS

*t*he truth is, we blow it. Most of us, on a daily basis. We let little things build up till we feel that familiar thunder rolling inside. We get a little snippy with that bank teller who is as slow as Christmas. We want to choke the cashier at the grocery story for closing the drawer *again* before giving us change. . . . We yell at our kids for no particular reason. We argue with our spouse and walk away mad. . . .

Remember playing childhood games? Nobody ever paid any attention to proper rules or regulations. If something didn't play out right, someone would yell, "Do over!" Well, with God, every day is a do-over day. We can beat our chest and moan and scream at ourselves all we want, but God has already said, "Do over!" One of the greatest challenges in our daily walk is accepting God's forgiveness. . . . If we have genuinely asked for forgiveness, then we've got it. Now we need to forgive ourselves.

DONNA VANLIERE
They Walked with Him

PROMISES TO
HELP YOU ACCEPT CHANGE

Whoever desires to save his life will lose it,
but whoever loses his life for My sake will save it.

LUKE 9:24

If any of you lacks wisdom,
let him ask of God, who gives to all
liberally and without reproach,
and it will be given to him.

JAMES 1:5

But we have this treasure in earthen vessels,
that the excellence of the power may
be of God and not of us.
We are hard-pressed on every side, yet not
crushed; we are perplexed, but not in despair.

2 CORINTHIANS 4:7–8

ACCEPTING CHANGES IN LIFE

Christmas dinner had long since ended and we were still visiting around the table.

"Why don't we go sit in the living room?" I suggested.

My sister-in-law quipped, "Because we fear change!"

We erupted in laughter over such a dramatic answer to my simple question. But there was a bit of truth in her humor.

Most of us feel a tinge of reluctance when it comes to change, because it means we must take a risk and release some of our control. . . .

We wrap ourselves around what we know and love and are reluctant to release. But if we cling to God's Word, then we are more willing to take risks in this life because we realize that we're made for adventure.

JENNIFER ROTHSCHILD
Lessons I Learned in the Light

PROMISES ABOUT
PLANNING FOR THE SABBATH

*Everyone who keeps from defiling the Sabbath,
and holds fast My covenant—even them
I will bring to My holy mountain, and make
them joyful in My house of prayer.*

ISAIAH 56:6–7

*The hour is coming, and now is,
when the true worshipers will worship the
Father in spirit and truth; for the Father is
seeking such to worship Him.*

JOHN 4:23

*Let the word of Christ dwell
in you richly in all wisdom, teaching and
admonishing one another in psalms
and hymns and spiritual songs, singing with
grace in your hearts to the Lord.*

COLOSSIANS 3:16

PLANNING FOR THE SABBATH

One of the most important aspects of Sabbath keeping is that we embrace intentionality. . . . Sabbath keeping says clearly that we are not going to do what everybody else does. We are going to be deliberate about our choices in order to live truly as we want to live in response to the grace of God. We are committed to certain values and, therefore, live in accordance with them as fully as we can. Everybody else catches up on yard work on Sundays, but we have chosen to rest from work on our Sabbath day. Everyone else goes window-shopping at the mall on that day, but we have chosen to cease the American hankering after possessions. . . .

We offer to the world the beauty of our lifestyles when we choose to be careful about each aspect of them.

MARVA DAWN
Morning by Morning

PROMISES ABOUT
CHOOSING TO BE GLAD

Oh, satisfy us early with Your mercy,
that we may rejoice
and be glad all our days!

PSALM 90:14

Let the righteous be glad;
let them rejoice before God.

PSALM 68:3

I have trusted in Your mercy;
my heart shall rejoice in Your salvation.

PSALM 13:5

Let all those rejoice
who put their trust in You.

PSALM 5:11

GLADNESS OR GRUMBLING?

*e*verywhere I turn today something tries to steal my joy. If I can't rejoice and be glad today, I will never rejoice and be glad. I will waste the joyous opportunities of today waiting for tomorrows that may or may not ever come. If I wait until life slows down, the sun comes back, the kids are older and less demanding, I lose some weight, my husband gets that raise, then I'll spend my life waiting rather than living and being glad.

The joys of life are found in and amongst life itself. Yes, life is full of frustrations, disappointments, pain, and suffering; but no matter what we are facing, having an attitude of joy will allow us to find the good that God promises us is there. If an oyster can make a pearl out of an irritating grain of sand, just think what you could do if in every situation you chose to rejoice!

LYSA TERKEURST
Living Life on Purpose

"Refrain your voice from weeping,
and your eyes from tears; for your work shall
be rewarded," says the LORD.

1 TIMOTHY 6:6

"I wish that all . . . were even as I myself.
But each one has his own gift from God, one in
this manner and another in that.
But I say to the unmarried and to the widows:
It is good for them if they
remain [single] even as I am."

1 CORINTHIANS 7:7–8

There is a difference between a wife
and a virgin. The unmarried woman cares
about the things of the Lord,
that she may be holy both in body and in spirit.
But she who is married cares about the things
of the world—how she may please her husband.

1 CORINTHIANS 7:34

SINGLE AND CONTENT

friends offer all sorts of advice to single women: don't be too aggressive or too backward, too friendly or too hard-to-get, too intellectual or too dumb, too earthy or too heavenly. Hang around till the bitter end of the singles' barbecue—he might want to take you home. Or, don't go to the singles' barbecue at all. Just stay home and read your Bible and pray. It's terribly confusing.

"Is my Father God in charge here or am I supposed to take over?" He is in charge if you want Him to be. He will not invade your freedom to choose to "take over." But if you want His way, nothing more, nothing less, and nothing *else*, you've got to leave it to Him. It's easy to be deceived here—telling ourselves we really want His will, but meaning "I want it so long as it includes marriage!"

God gives the very best to those who leave the choice with Him.

ELISABETH ELLIOT
Keep a Quiet Heart

The LORD is near to all who call upon Him,
to all who call upon Him in truth.

PSALM 145:18

While I live I will praise the LORD;
I will sing praises to my God
while I have my being.

PSALM 146:2

Let the hearts of those rejoice
who seek the Lord! Seek the Lord and His
strength; seek His face evermore!

PSALM 105:3–4

THE WONDER
OF WORSHIPING GOD

i watched one year as the Academy of Motion
Pictures gave a special award to a veteran actor.
Before he was invited to take the stage, we were
treated to a brief overview of his prestigious career.
Many of his industry colleagues praised his work.
As he walked onto the stage the applause was
deafening; he stood for a few moments enjoying
the support of his community. Eventually the
clapping subsided, but before he was able to make
his speech the music played him off. *Sorry, time's up.*
It was clear that he wanted to respond but the
evening had moved on.

I think sometimes we do the same in our
worship. We love to tell God how much we adore
Him, how He has changed our lives. We revel in
the tidal waves of song, but then "time's up" and we
move on. If we would just wait on God, let the
silence fall, we could be gifted with the response of
a loving Father to His children. In that holy
moment we could receive a blessing that no human
words could begin to frame.

SHEILA WALSH

The Best Devotions of Sheila Walsh

PROMISES ABOUT
THE JOY OF GOD'S WORD

The judgments of the LORD are true
and righteous altogether.
More to be desired are they than gold,
yea, than much fine gold;
sweeter also than honey and the honeycomb.

PSALM 19:9–10

How sweet are Your words to my taste,
sweeter than honey to my mouth!

PSALM 119:103

I will delight myself
in Your commandments, which I love.

PSALM 119:47

THE JOY OF GOD'S WORD

*f*ood makes me happy. Some of my favorite food memories include . . .

Dipping Oreo cookies in milk at midnight with Daddy.

Mom and I stuffing ourselves with Senora Martinez' tacos in Progresso, Mexico.

Eating approximately 972 Shanghai dumplings in Shanghai, China with my husband.

Crisp mornings of fresh scrambled eggs (lots of salt) with my son.

For me, good company enriches any meal. And Jeremiah felt the same way. His favorite food was God's Word in the company of . . . God Himself!

What an incredible banquet God gives us through His Word. . . . Food may make us happy for a moment. God's Word gives us joy for a lifetime!

ALICIA BRITT CHOLE
Pure Joy

PROMISES ABOUT
DOING THE WORK OF GOD

*He who believes in Me,
the works that I do he will do also; and greater
works than these he will do.*

JOHN 14:12

*"If anyone loves Me, he will keep My word;
and My Father will love him, and We will come
to him and make Our home with him."*

JOHN 14:23

*Let the beauty of the LORD our God be upon us,
and establish the work of our hands for us;
yes, establish the work of our hands.*

PSALM 90:17

Doing the Work of God

ears ago, I read that the average woman today has the equivalent of *fifty* full-time servants, in the form of modern, timesaving devices and equipment. That figure may or may not be accurate, but we certainly have many conveniences available to us that were unknown to women of past generations. Imagine going back to the days when there were no dishwashers, microwaves, washing machines, dryers, or automobiles. . . .

So why are our lives more harried and hurried than ever? Why are we so stressed out? . . .

In Jesus' words, we find a clue—a powerful Truth that sets us free from the bondage of hurry and frustration about all we have to do. Notice what work Jesus completed in the thirty-three years He was here on the earth: "I have finished the work *which thou gavest me to do*" (John 17:4 KJV). That is the secret. Jesus didn't finish everything His disciples wanted Him to do. . . . He didn't finish everything the multitudes wanted Him to do. . . . But He did finish the work that *God* gave Him to do.

NANCY LEIGH DEMOSS

Lies Women Believe

PROMISES ABOUT
SPIRITUAL GROWTH

*Grow in the grace and knowledge
of our Lord and Savior Jesus Christ.*

2 PETER 3:18

*We all, with unveiled face,
beholding as in a mirror the glory of the Lord,
are being transformed into
the same image from glory to glory,
just as by the Spirit of the Lord.*

2 CORINTHIANS 3:18

*Become blameless and pure,
children of God without fault in a crooked
and depraved generation.*

PHILIPPIANS 2:15 NIV

*Keep your heart with all diligence,
for out of it spring the issues of life.*

PROVERBS 4:23

GROWING SPIRITUALLY

*t*rue knowledge of Christ comes only as we are willing to give up our dreams of glory, praying to be identified with Him on the cross. . . . Are we really willing to let God take us through times of defeat and despair, when we experience communion with Him in His crucifixion?

The wonder of God's goodness is that He can use these "crosses" for our sanctification, just as He used the death of Jesus to advance His redemptive plan. "You meant evil against me, but God meant it for good," Joseph told his brothers (Gen. 50:20). Christians sometimes think it a matter of piety to deny the evil done to them—to cover it up, say it wasn't so bad, wear a smile in public. But Joseph did not shrink from calling his brothers' actions *evil*, and neither should we. In this world, we too will be rejected by people with sinful motives, and for the sake of truth we should call it what it is. But we can also turn it to good by realizing that suffering gives us a chance to enter spiritually upon the journey that Jesus mapped out for us: rejected, slain (spiritually), and, finally, raised.

NANCY PEARCEY
Total Truth

"In the world you will have tribulation:
but be of good cheer, I have overcome the world."

JOHN 16:33

He shall cover you with His feathers,
and under His wings you shall take refuge.

PSALM 91:4

Commit your way to the LORD,
trust also in Him, and He shall bring it to pass.
He shall bring forth your righteousness
as the light, and your justice as the noonday.

PSALM 37:5–6

God Is In Control

One morning my computer simply would not obey me. What a nuisance. I had my work laid out, my timing figured, my mind all set. My work was delayed, my timing thrown off, my thinking interrupted. Then I remembered. It was not for nothing. This was part of the Plan (not mine, His). "Lord, You have assigned me my portion and my cup."

Now if the interruption had been a human being instead of an infuriating mechanism, it would not have been so hard to see it as the most important part of the work of the day. But *all* is under my Father's control: yes, recalcitrant computers, faulty transmissions, drawbridges which happen to be up when one is in a hurry. My portion. My cup. My lot is secure. My heart can be at peace. My Father is in charge. How simple!

ELISABETH ELLIOT
Keep a Quiet Heart

Acknowledgments

Grateful acknowledgment is made to the following
publishers for permission to reprint this copyrighted
material.

June Masters Bacher, *Quiet Moments for Women.* Eugene,
Or.: Harvest House, 1979.

June Masters Bacher, *The Quiet Heart.* Eugene, Or.:
Harvest House, 1988.

Julie Ann Barnhill, *Exquisite Hope: The Something More
You've Been Longing For!* Wheaton: Tyndale House,
2005.

Julie Ann Barnhill, *Scandalous Grace: Celebrate the
Liberating and Tantalizing Realities of Divine Grace.*
Wheaton: Tyndale House, 2004.

Corrie ten Boom, *Messages of God's Abundance.* Grand
Rapids: Zondervan, 2002.

Jill Briscoe, *Heartstrings: Finding a Song When You've Lost
Your Joy.* Wheaton, Ill: Tyndale House, 1997.

Jill Briscoe, *Quiet Times with God.* Wheaton, Ill: Tyndale
House, 1997.

Jill Briscoe, *Women in the Life of Jesus.* Colorado Springs:
Chariot Victor Publishing, 1986.

Patsy Clairmont, *Mending Your Heart in a Broken World.*
New York: Warner Books, 2001.

Alicia Britt Chole, *Pure Joy*, Nashville, J Countryman,
2003.

Alicia Britt Chole, *Sitting in God's Sunshine, Resting in
His Love.* Nashville, J Countryman, 2005.

Marva Dawn, *Morning by Morning.* Grand Rapids:
Eerdmans Publishing Co., 2001.

Marva Dawn, *To Walk and Not Faint: A Month of Meditations on Isaiah 40.* Grand Rapids: Eerdmans Publishing Co., 1997.

Nancy Leigh DeMoss, *Lies Women Believe and the Truth That Sets Them Free.* Chicago: Moody, Press, 2001.

Elisabeth Elliot, *Keep a Quiet Heart.* Ann Arbor, Mich.: Servant Books, 1995.

Elisabeth Elliot, *God's Guidance.* Grand Rapids: Fleming H. Revell, 1997.

Elisabeth Elliot, *On Asking God Why.* Grand Rapids: Fleming H. Revell, 1989.

Denise George, *Cultivating a Forgiving Heart.* Grand Rapids: Zondervan, 2004.

Laurie Beth Jones, *Jesus in Blue Jeans.* New York: Hyperion, 1997.

Carol Kent, *Secret Longings of the Heart: Overcoming Deep Disappointment and Unfulfilled Expectations.* Colorado Springs: NavPress, 2003.

Anne Graham Lotz, *I Saw the Lord: A Wake-Up Call for Your Heart.* Grand Rapids: Zondervan, 2006.

Catherine Marshall, *A Closer Walk.* New York: Avon Books, 1986.

Sharon Jaynes and Lysa Terkeurst, *A Woman's Secret to a Balanced Life,* Eugene: Harvest House, 2004.

Stormie Omartian, *The Power of a Praying Wife,* Eugene: Harvest House, 1997.

Nancy Pearcy, *Total Truth: Liberating Christianity from Its Cultural Captivity.* Wheaton: Crossway Books, 2004.

Anita Renfroe, *The Purse-Driven Life: It Really Is All About Me*, Colorado Springs: NavPress, 2005.

Jennifer Rothschild, *Lessons I Learned in the Light: All You Need to Thrive in a Dark World.* Sisters: Multnomah Publishers, 2006.

Jennifer Rothschild, *Lessons I Learned in the Dark: Steps to Walking by Faith, Not by Sight*. Sisters: Multnomah Publishers, 2002.

Jan Silvious, *Moving Beyond the Myths: Hope and Encouragement for Women*. Chicago: Moody Press, 2001.

Jan Silvious, *Look at It This Way: Straightforward Wisdom to Put Life in Perspective*. Colorado Springs: WaterBrook Press, 2003.

Joni Eareckson Tada, *Diamonds in the Dust*. Grand Rapids, Zondervan, 1993.

Lysa TerKeurst, *Living Life on Purpose*. Chicago: Moody Press, 2000.

Lysa TerKeurst, *Radically Obedient, Radically Blessed: Experiencing God in Extraordinary Ways*. Eugene: Harvest House Publishers, 2003.

Ingrid Trobisch, *Hidden Strength*. Minneapolis: MacAlester Park Publishing Company, 1996.

Donna VanLiere, *They Walked with Him: Stories of Those Who Knew Him Best*. Louisiana: Howard Publishing, 2001.

Sheila Walsh, *The Best Devotions of Sheila Walsh*. Grand Rapids: Zondervan, 2001.

Jan Winebrenner, *Intimate Faith: A Woman's Guide to the Spiritual Disciplines*. New York: Warner Books, 2003.

Christine Wood, *Character Witness*. Downers Grove: Intervarsity Press, 2003.

Women of Faith, *Boundless Love,* Grand Rapids, Zondervan, 2001.

Women of Faith, *Extravagant Grace,* Grand Rapids, Zondervan, 2000.